'This has been my best week in a very, ver
last session I have felt more clarity on a
felt 'stuck' in my eating/binging cycle. I
control of my life and my body and, best
free.'

Teresa S.

'Geoff, I'd like to say thank you for the amazing change you've brought about and I am on an emotional high. Just one session has had an impact on me; I now think in terms of "I am worthy of ... " or "It's reasonable for me to have X or Y need fulfilled" which is certainly not what my internal mental dialogue was before.'

Ian M.

'Thank you so much Geoff - I really thought I was slowly going mental! Your words are exactly what I needed today. I'm going to read and re-read them (and perhaps print them out and stick them on my mirror at home!). I really appreciate it - thanks again.'

Rebecca A.

'On World Mental Health Day, I have to do a massive shoutout to the best life coach, Geoff Sober. Thank you for telling me I'm a good mum and getting me back to some sort of normal.'

Abbie C.

'Kerry and I got loads of value from your coaching. Equally, we enjoyed your keeping us accountable each week with our Skype call. This really helped to keep us focussed on the high leveraged actions we needed to take weekly in order for us to achieve, keeping us focussed on "the one thing".

Thanks also for the breakthroughs you enabled me to have through some of the one-to-one sessions, where we worked on clearing 'blockers'. This really blew me away and I felt so liberated - the weight was removed from my shoulders. Thank you so much for your passion, enthusiasm and encouragement.'

Martin M.

'I just wanted to say that I felt instantly better after our session. I still feel very relaxed about what I have to do.

Maryanne M.

'Working with Geoff has been a great pleasure and he has always helped me to be the best me I can be, through attending his workshops and one-to-one mentorship.

Wayne M.

Geoff Sober

From
Fear of Failure
to
Flying High

Contact Geoff at:
support@blankcanvastraining.com
Website: geoffsober.com

I dedicate this book to the people I love most:

My dearest wife Sue - your unwavering loyalty, love and support has kept me strong when I felt weak.
I love you.

My incredible children, Christopher and Clare - as children you lit up my life and now, as adults, I could not be prouder of the wonderful human beings you are.

My amazing grandchildren, Hallie May, Ben and Rory - thank you for playing with me. You remind me to laugh, love life and have fun. You are treasures.

Be yourself; everyone else is taken.

Oscar Wilde (attrib.)

Contents

Foreword

I'd been mentoring and coaching for 18 years when I got a WhatsApp message from an old friend of mine who said, 'So, Geoff, where can I get a copy of your book?' which was embarrassing because I hadn't written it yet!

So here it is at last – the story of my journey 'from fear of failure to flying high'. If I can do it, anyone can.

Introduction

Do you often feel like everybody you know is living their best life? They're all *'#smashingit'* on social media with the dream job/home/family, while you haven't managed to move off the starting line? That's certainly a feeling that was *very* familiar to me.

Now, more than ever, we are aware of so many windows into the lives of others: people we know well, some we've only just met, and then, of course, there are all the celebrities and influencers. And so, we clear a little circle in the glass and peer through.

What stopped *us* from taking that job we really wanted? Why didn't we head out on on that adventure or take that chance on love? Why have others succeeded where we have failed?

In my work as a life coach, I find that I attract clients who have encountered similar issues to those that blocked me in achieving my goals; the same barriers; the same doubts; the same negative attitudes. I've worked very successfully with these clients over the years; coaching, supporting, and sharing my own experiences along the way, in order to help them reach their full potential. It wasn't until recently, however, that I started to dig a little deeper into the influences that had shaped my own 'fear of failure'. Where did my barriers come from? When did they first appear – and why? My coaching methods were effective, but I wanted to understand more about the 'psychology' behind that success.

I realised that the question I was trying to answer was this: *What exactly am I an expert in...?* I'd worked with my many clients very effectively without ever having fully explored the aetiology of my own initial fears. I found the answer during a conversation I had with Jon Street, a marketing expert. I was telling him how I had been held back in achieving my goals by what I perceived to be a general lack of confidence, or apathy, when he told me: 'Your story is all about overcoming the fear of failure.'

He nailed it, right there on the spot, which was a real 'light-bulb moment' for me. I realised that I'd wrestled with the concept of 'failure' throughout my teenage years and into early adulthood. Before becoming a life coach, I'd been afraid to talk about my 'failures', never wanting to open up about things that had gone wrong in my life and the opportunities that had passed me by, but all that changed once I managed to overcome my fears.

Now, I find that the more I discuss 'fear of failure' and open up about my life, the more I see that – my goodness – this fear of failure is *everywhere!* Those people who aren't making it in life; who aren't where they want to be, or where they always assumed or hoped they would be, are experiencing a fear of failure.

Finding the root of my fear of failure meant turning back to my childhood. So many of our patterns in life come from our parents, and this is a theme that runs through my story.

I was very close to my father; a clever man whom I loved dearly. People often remarked on how we looked and even sounded alike. After he passed away, I was clearing out his home when I came across some old hand-made boardgames he had created. There was a football game with all the individual pieces carefully drafted out – he was such a detailed man – and another, really clever, beautifully-made game similar to Monopoly. Neither of these games had ever seen the light of day or made it out into the world. Why? Because of my father's fear of failure; his fear of putting himself out there; of being rejected; of other people's opinions – he had so many fears.

Sometime after clearing out the house, I attended a coaching session where the discussion revolved around 'finding your passion'. We were told the answer lay in pinpointing *What makes you cry?* Straightaway I knew it was this: my father's boardgames; so cleverly thought out and beautifully made – hidden away, covered in dust.

In order to overcome our fear of failure, we need to go further than just recognising the symptoms – we need to take action, and, crucially, *continue* taking action. In this book I will talk about how, by taking action, I was able to move forward and start achieving my goals, from recognising I was in the wrong profession, to achieving my lifetime ambition of owning a successful business… and so much more. Because achieving goals isn't just about business and money. We all strive for a happy life, which holistically means happy friendships, strong relationships, and good health. All these goals are important, and I've made them happen – by taking *action*.

Some years ago, I was talking to a fellow life coach – a highly motivational speaker who attracted audiences of around 70 or more – who asked me, 'How many people out of these 70 do you think actually take inspiration from my talks and go on to be a success?'

I took what I thought was a pretty conservative guess, 'Ten?' I suggested. 'Twelve, maybe?'

'Two,' he replied. I was really taken aback; stunned, in fact, because he was a very powerful speaker.

'But why?' The question went round in my head for a while, until it dawned on me that I knew the answer. Of course I did! I'd been that person in the audience, in fact, I was quite a self-help 'junkie' at one point, going to all the talks and reading all the books. Yet nothing in my life changed.

Why? Because in striving to achieve our goals, we start to make all the right moves, focussing on the end goal which, we are told, is just ahead of us. A beckoning light at the end of the tunnel. Only the tunnel is long, and the light is far away, and as time passes, life intervenes, the light grows dim and the tunnel seems to stretch even farther into the distance. We might begin the journey, but it isn't long before we get distracted, or daunted, and give up. That is, until we pick up the next self-help book, or go to the next talk; then off we go again, searching for hope.

These are what Dusan Djukich refers to in his book *Straight-line Leadership* as 'circle people' – those who go round and round in a vicious circle of inactivity. They constantly seek out the next motivational speaker or newly released self-help book in an effort to rekindle the flame ignited at the last talk they went to, or book they read. Then back they come to reality – the cynic in the office and the doubters amongst friends – and that flame splutters and quickly dies. Circle people live their lives caught in an inescapable loop, moving from motivation to apathy and back again.

The second group of people that Djukich identifies are those who get some way towards achieving their goals, before falling by the wayside. Often these goals are suggested to them by others, so the motivation is weak from the outset. Djukich calls them 'zigzaggers' as they steer themselves towards positive change, they might even take a positive action, but turn back as soon as they meet an obstacle, rather than looking for a solution. These people revert to their old ways until the next opportunity presents itself, which they will attempt to seize, before ultimately giving up again... and so that pattern continues. In the end, of course, it's easier just to stay put.

Finally, there are the people who embrace the concept of personal growth – *and make it happen.* Djukich calls them the 'straight-liners'; those who have identified a way forward which they reach by consistently taking one step at a time, without turning back or abandoning hope. Action follows action until they arrive at the place they want to be.

Becoming a 'straight-liner' was my salvation. It's how I went from a job that stifled my ambition and gave me little satisfaction, to achieving my dream of owning and running a highly successful business. I didn't focus on the end goal, instead I pushed forward one step at a time until I was where *I* wanted to be. However... before taking that first step, I had to overcome what I now realise was my deep-seated fear of failure.

From Fear of Failure to Flying High is not just a candid, personal account of my own journey to success, it's about showing others how they too can recognise fear of failure in themselves and gather the weapons to fight it.

PART 1

~ 1 ~

Learning to Fear

I firmly believe that each of us is the product of our upbringing. As Philip Larkin famously wrote:

> They fuck you up, your mum and dad,
> They may not mean to, but they do.
> They fill you with the faults they had
> And add some extra, just for you.

It's a well-documented fact that children learn to fear from a very early age and that, by the time they are seven, many will have amassed a significant collection of worries –

some of them quite impressive – most of which they will have learned from their parents. *[There is a large body of literature indicating that parents can transmit fears to their children by sharing their fearful thoughts, stories, warnings and biases: (Creswell, Shildreick, & Field, 2011; Drake & Ginsburg, 2012; Muris & Field, 2010).]*

My parents were the sort who wanted a quiet life. My father, Arthur, had a difficult time as a teenager, the effects of which, I'm convinced, spilled into his adulthood. He contracted tuberculosis and spent two years in a sanitorium, where, alone for the majority of his stay, he passed his time reading. I can't gauge the impact that had on him, all I can say is that the man I knew was deeply affected by his difficult upbringing. His illness left him physically weak with asthma and a bad chest. I suspect this contributed in no small way to his being introverted and preferring his own company to that of others.

Both he and my mother were quite closed-off individuals who didn't like to delve into the unpleasant parts of their past, so I have only ever gleaned small details about his life. However, I know that as a child, and even into adulthood, he was quiet and withdrawn, moving from school to work, and then from job to job, without making any ripples in the universe.

I wish I'd known more about my father's early life as the small amount of information I do have is quite intriguing. He was an only child who suffered significant trauma when his mother 'disappeared' for a year or so. The whole episode was apparently very scandalous, even making the newspapers at the time. The details are very vague and apparently, she left without leaving so much as a note. I can only assume she went to live with another man for a time. It was all very embarrassing, and deeply upsetting for the family, not least my father who never forgave her. Their relationship suffered very badly after she returned home and, sadly, was never mended.

My mother, Dorothy, lived in the shadow of her elder brother who was not only very academic, but was also a highly talented musician. I always got the feeling that, as a girl, her parents assumed she wanted nothing more in life than to marry, have children and become a housewife. She did, however, have a burning ambition to be a nurse and managed to get an interview at Bensham General Hospital in Gateshead. She was only 17 at the time, and so brought her own mother along with her for support. The matron conducting the interview told my mother, 'You'll never become a nurse because you're too sensitive and care too much about people's feelings. You'll take on everybody's problems and be no good to us at all. You need to be tougher.' Or words to that effect.

I can picture it now, my teenage mother crumbling tearfully under the stern words of the matron, backed up by her own mother who, I'm sure, would have said something like, 'Well, that's that then.' There certainly wouldn't have been any encouragement to try again when she was older or work harder to achieve her goal. Having failed to follow her own dreams, my mother would wax lyrical about all the 'the poets and musicians' in the family in order to satisfy her need for self-worth.

Then there was her grandfather, William Murray, who owned a very successful undertaker's business in Gateshead. He was quite the entrepreneur and had a lot of social standing in the local community. As the eldest of my generation within the family, I do have some vague recollections of meeting him. In fact, my mother used to tell me I resembled him, although I suspect that her comments may have had more to do with maternal pride than anything else!

As well as being a successful business-owner, my great-grandfather was also an accomplished athlete – rumour has it that he was the best sprinter in Gateshead. He lived in an imposing Victorian house, where various members of the family would visit him for help and advice in sorting out their problems; some of which he solved by lending money, others by handing out jobs within his business.

William Murray was very much the patriarch, and I always knew from the way my mother spoke about her grandfather that she very much admired and looked up to him, although I wonder if his power had the effect of weakening the other men in the family?

When William Murray eventually retired, he offered the family business to his son-in-law (my mother's father) who turned it down. I feel sure this decision was based on his fear of failure; his belief that he would never be able to live up to the reputation of his father-in-law.

Interestingly, I once had quite a heart-to-heart with my mother where she said, 'I'm worried I've made all of you [meaning me and my two brothers] the way you are.' She went on to tell me how terribly afraid she had been of being pregnant and having to raise a child, and that she'd always felt that she wouldn't be a good enough mother. Indeed, throughout my childhood she would blame herself for everything she perceived as going wrong – from my school grades to my developing childhood eczema which turned into asthma.

I was always rather sickly when I was young and, very early on, her worries transferred themselves onto me, not least because I was the first child.

And so here may well lie the foundation stones of fear, including fear of failure, low self-esteem and the inability to express one's talents in the world.

My mother came from a family of teachers and headteachers who, because of my great-grandfather's wealth and standing, would have been considered upper middle class. My father, on the other hand, would have been looked upon by them as lower middle class, perhaps even working class. His father, my grandfather, was a painter and decorator – a very modest occupation in their eyes – and I suspect this class disparity would have caused problems for my parents when it was announced to the family that they wanted to get married.

Whilst my father might have had a 'run-of-the-mill' job, he was a very intelligent man and the story goes that when my mother's family played parlour games, he would win them all. Having spent those two years in the sanitorium reading, he became something of a polymath and in later life, if he went to a pub quiz or played Trivial Pursuit, he always won hands-down.

My father never bragged about being good at anything, that wasn't his way, although he was quietly competitive and would never let us win at things like table tennis or pool when we were children. He even created a tennis club in the village and when it came to competition time, the general consensus was always along the lines of: *You might as well take the trophy now, Arthur, because we all know you're going to win it anyway!* He was that good. My brothers and I used to play against him, and he would thrash us all out of the park. When I look back now, it pains me to think that he never brought that competitive spirit out into the world. There was an air of resignation about him which, I now believe, was something he used to mask his unwillingness to face his fears.

My father's life certainly wasn't without its opportunities, and in the mid-1960s he went for an interview for an accountancy job at the new international sports centre at Crystal Palace. It would have been the perfect opportunity for him, combining his key strengths of attention to detail, organisation and sport, in a very exciting venture.

His talents were recognised and he was offered the job – but turned it down. I tried talking to him about his decision but, along with so many other things, it was a subject he didn't want to discuss; not with me, and not even with my mother. He could never talk openly about his disappointments or failures. I know that accepting the position would have entailed his moving the family 'down south', and I suspect that presented a challenge he was simply too afraid to face.

Until I was seven, we lived in the centre of Gateshead, just outside Newcastle, where my father worked as an auditor for a furniture company called Hardy's. At that time, I was the blue-eyed boy and was top of my class. I was very happy at the local primary school, where I had lots of friends, all of whom lived nearby, so I could see them after school and at weekends.

However, as Gateshead became more urbanised, my parents decided that moving out to the countryside would give us all a better life, particularly me and my brothers. My father started working for the National Trust – where he was to spend the rest of his career – and we moved from the city to the tiny Northumbrian village of Scots Gap.

One of the main benefits of a job with the National

Trust is being able to live in one of their properties which, as you might imagine, was lovely. So, there we were, living in National Trust splendour in the northeast, but on a relatively modest income. We had all the appearances of wealth, just without the money, and I always had the sense that we were just about getting by and that my ordinary parents were living a life of 'wealth by proxy', rather like my mother's 'fame by proxy' when she talked about the poets and musicians in her family.

Telling friends that my father worked for the National Trust always sounded very impressive and during the course of his career he did, indeed, come into contact with many of the landed gentry. Our house bordered West Grange Hall, the country house and estate owned by Lady Wendy Lycett, heiress to the Colman's Mustard fortune. My mother knew Lady Wendy through the Women's Institute – all the local women did.

We always knew when Lady Wendy was on the phone because my mother would use her posh telephone voice, as did my father when he spoke to anybody he considered to be upper class. It wasn't that he wanted to impress particularly, he just wanted to fit in. I now understand how that impacted my and my brother's behaviours as we were taught to fit in with the people around us. We weren't shown how to have an identity of our own, instead we followed our parents' example by diluting down who and what we were in deference to making others feel comfortable.

The precise nature of my father's job was always a slightly grey area in that it fell somewhere between accountancy and management. He 'looked after' various National Trust properties in the northeast, overseeing the staff as well as managing the accounts. One property I particularly remember was Wallington Hall, owned by the Trevelyan family who still have a presence within the Conservative Party (Anne-Marie Trevelyan). Another was a house called Cragside, built by the visionary inventor, William George Armstrong, an engineer and businessman in the 19th century. It was an impressive place, being most heralded as the first house in the world to have lights powered by hydroelectricity.

The National Trust has various properties dotted all around the country where, at that time, employees could live for little or no rent. This meant my parents spent their lives moving between National Trust houses whilst never actually owning a home of their own. In their later years, they moved from Scots Gap to another, larger, house called The Old Vicarage in Cambo, barely a mile away.

Once again, my parents achieved respect and standing in the community, not through their innate talents or skills, but by proxy. If you worked for the National Trust and lived in a big house then a modicum of respectability was afforded you. Thereby my parents devolved themselves of the responsibility to make more of their lives.

My father was 'retired' from the National Trust after 35 years of service, three years ahead of his planned leaving date. He and my mother then moved again, this time to a smaller National Trust home. Sadly, leaving his job too soon and moving to the smaller house all but killed him. The layers of pretence that my parents had built-up over the years began to peel away, and from the age of 62 he went into a rapid physical decline, eventually passing away at 75.

The National Trust had been his whole life and his respectability, but just like all the houses he lived in, everything was only ever borrowed.

~ 2 ~

Rebel Without a Clue

I had been very happy living in the city, however our move out to the countryside and my father starting work for the National Trust marked the beginning of change.

My parents decided that the local village school, attended mainly by the children from nearby farms, wasn't good enough for me. They put a lot of importance on education and so decided instead to send me to a larger school which was 12 miles away in Morpeth.

Although I was fairly happy at primary school, being so far away from home meant that I never felt part of the local community. Still… I was bright and good at sports, so things weren't too bad at that stage.

My parents were very keen for me to pass the 11+ so that I could go to the King Edward VI grammar school in Morpeth. I was successful in passing the exam, but the move to grammar school was the beginning of a very unhappy period in my life. Once again, none of the friends I made at school lived in the same village as me, which was an hour away. I used to get the bus home at four o'clock every afternoon, while everyone else stayed on at school to attend the various sports clubs, or to just meet up and hang out together.

I felt like a total outsider. I didn't belong with the kids at school because I never spent any quality time with them, and I had no friends where we lived because they were 'villagers' and I was a 'townie'. I arrived home from school every evening to a largely empty house, although as my brothers grew older – there is a four-year age gap between each of us – one of them was occasionally around to provide some company.

I went from being quite a sociable child at primary school, to a complete loner by the time I was 12. Perhaps some of my unhappiness was to do with my entering the 'teenage years'? I'm not sure. I do, however, know for certain that moving away from Gateshead, then attending a school so far from home that I couldn't see my friends, made the situation far, far worse.

Looking back, I think of my teenage years as being incredibly lonely. By the time I was 13, I had morphed from a gregarious extrovert into a solitary introvert. I *hated* the countryside, and I *hated* the house. 'I'd rather we lived in a Gateshead slum than here!' I told my father.

Surprisingly, neither of my brothers felt the same way, which is something we talked about fairly recently. 'Oh, you hated it there, didn't you?' said my younger brother Richard. Inasmuch as I couldn't understand him being happy, he couldn't understand my misery. Thanks to his country upbringing, my brother now lives very happily in splendid isolation in North Yorkshire. His home is so remote you'd think he was permanently isolating from a pandemic.

My unhappiness and loneliness grew into anger and rebellion. I decided that all my teachers were stupid and I spent most of my secondary education playing truant.

My parents, who had no idea how to handle me, threw up their hands in despair. The complete lack of communication in our family only served to make matters worse. There was no openness and anyone feeling miserable or aggrieved showed their feelings by sulking alone in a room, staying quiet and moody and hoping things would magically change. Not surprisingly, they didn't.

Turning inwards became my identity. I was more comfortable being on my own with my thoughts, and thinking became my refuge from the world. I can now see how this has benefited me as I coach myself and others, Pondering life's mysteries is one of my greatest pleasures. On the other hand, this introspection fuelled my fear of stepping out into the world in case I might be judged or seen for who I thought I was.

I became quite adept at skipping school and my usual modus operandi involved taking the school bus to Morpeth, then hitch-hiking back home to spend the day alone, once I knew my parents were both safely out of the house. Sometimes my friend Iain would play truant with me and we would sit together in the park, fantasising about a future where we set up our own business or travelled the world. Like me, Iain also went on to be a business owner. In retrospect, our teenage dreams turned out to be quite prophetic!

When I was 16, I was sent off to a careers adviser at school whose first words to me were: 'Before I give you any careers advice, attending lessons might be a start to your getting somewhere in life.' He then went on to suggest that I learn to type and join the army, neither of which sounded particularly appealing, although with hindsight the typing would have been useful.

I got a major wake-up call when it came to taking my 'O' levels. It's hard to admit, even now, but I had a certain arrogance about me when it came to teachers and studying. It went something along the lines of, *I'm better than all of this, but I don't need to prove it.*

This is a trait I have noticed amongst my mentees. Quite often those who fear failure have an inward-looking confidence which almost verges on arrogance. The inner frustration of not stepping out and fulfilling one's talent stimulates an anger which smugly states: *I know I'm better than you all think I am, only I'm too scared to step out of the shadows and take the actions which would prove my abilities.*

Despite skipping most of my classes, I honestly thought that I would breeze through the exams. Homework and studying were for everybody else, but not me.

In the event, I took nine subjects and passed only five. It was probably the first time, in terms of education, that I felt a real sting of disappointment – maybe even regret? I'd never done any homework, so what did I expect? I remember the blasé feeling of *I don't care* and *So what?* But it turned out that I did care.

My parents, who must have been upset, kept their feelings to themselves. Perhaps they were simply resigned to the fact that I was going to get poor grades, knowing that I'd put in no effort whatsoever?

Having done so poorly in my 'O' levels, and having made no secret of the fact that I hated school, I was given the opportunity to leave at 16. But then came the fear of, *Now what?* So I stayed on and re-did my German 'O' level, working harder this time and managing to pass. I found that learning modern languages came naturally to me and that I was quite good at them.

When it came to 'A' levels, I started out studying for three but somehow managed to drop one along the way without anyone noticing. Everything I did was about getting by with the least amount of effort. I decided that if I couldn't succeed through sheer talent, then I simply mustn't be any good.

I still think of myself as the embodiment of the 'lazy teenager', but deep down I know that I was quite afraid and confused. I look back at that time with a sense of how truly awful it all was and how I felt there was a big hole in my life. I wasted so much of my young life sitting around, either listening to music or watching tv, when I could have been working hard to reach my goals. But then, what were my goals? I had no sense of direction and no place I needed to be. When the time came for me to actually take my 'A' level exams, the school informed my parents that they would have to foot the bill as my attendance record was so poor.

It wasn't until I was in my late 20s to early 30s, that I finally felt this pressing need to make up for those lost years. If you were to ask my wife now about my working habits, she'd say that I was a workaholic. My old business partner would have said the same, because there I would be, still working away in the office at seven o'clock in the evening, determined to get something finished when everyone else had gone home.

At this point, I should say that my one saving grace through those teenage years was that I was happy to work for money. My father got me a job as a woodsman for the

National Trust at Wallington Hall from the age of 13 and I earned £6.50 a week during the school holidays. I discovered I had quite a strong work ethic, if I was getting paid, and I managed to save all the money I earned.

Despite ridiculing and belittling teachers for the entirety of my teenage years, I ironically went straight from school to teacher training college. I was starting to fear for my future and had no original ideas on what I might do or who I might become.

My parents had 'stayed small' in the world and when my time came, they passed the baton of hiding and avoiding any chance of upset down to me. Their vision of my future was simple: I would live in a small village near to them, have a steady, reliable job with a pension plan, then get married and have the requisite 2.4 children. Staying safe and keeping my head below the parapet was the extent of their ambition on my behalf.

However, something inside told me that where I was headed was all wrong. There was a fire inside me, but fear kept it effectively doused. Nevertheless, my parents' fears for my future had become my fears so, with seemingly no other option, I took the path of least resistance.

~ 3 ~

Student Life

Having managed to scrape 'A' levels in French and German, I was presented with three opportunities: to try and get into teacher training college – and it would be a low-rate college because my 'A' levels weren't particularly good; spend some time in either France or Germany to improve my language skills; or get a job.

When you fear failure – when you've been taught to stay safe and not risk defeat – you choose the easy option. I had been in education for most of my life, so I stayed in education despite hating that very institution. Truth be told, I could not make a decision as to what to do after school and so my parents contacted my uncle who was a lecturer in a college of education. He pulled a few strings with colleagues of his and, without my having to do a thing, I was enrolled at Northumberland College of Education, a teacher training college approximately 20 minutes away from my parents' house. Laziness, apathy, and the absence of an adventurous spirit ensured I upheld the family pattern of avoiding risk.

I lived in halls for the first year and went home every weekend; that's how insular I'd become. As time went by, however, I started to make friends and become more sociable. The whole experience was quite an awakening for me – I started playing football and ran the team.

One of my highlights was organising a big weekend of social events at the college, which included a punk band called Coils IUD, as well as a fancy-dress extravaganza and a hypnotist show.

I also happened to book a band by the name of Last Exit for the Friday night. They were a sort of jazz/rock band and were undoubtedly a cut above the usual bands that the college hired. I went to pay this band their £60 for the night's entertainment and I recall how dejected they looked as I thanked them. They were obviously an ambitious, talented band, sick of playing to students who were too drunk to appreciate their quality. The lead singer was Gordon Sumner, better known to you as Sting, who went on to become one of the biggest stars in the music industry as he headed up The Police.

The weekend was a massive hit and a real lightbulb moment for me. I thought, *Wow! I can actually do things!* At the end of the evening I was called up onto the stage where I was thanked by representatives of the College Union. Instead of returning their thanks, and in the spirit of punk, I told the assembled masses that they were all 'f*#king crap' and next time they had better show up. I remember shocking myself as I couldn't figure out where this had come from. Something was stirring and it felt great.

My weekend visits home dwindled as I started to enjoy myself on campus and, while I didn't exactly throw myself into the academic side of things, I started to come round to the idea that I needed to put in at least some effort. It was a four-year course, and by the fourth year I was burning the midnight oil, working hard to catch up after all the partying of my first three years, although I don't think I was alone in that!

It was in my final year that I met the girl who is now my wife.

Sue grew up in a well-to-do family from around Glasgow. Her father had been a captain in the merchant navy and there were lots of creative people in the family; actual poets and musicians, as opposed to the ethereal, long-gone ancestors of my mother's stories.

I got to experience a different kind of life being with Sue, which really grew me as a person, in the same way that I think a lot of men 'grow up' once they are in a serious relationship. It gives them a bit of direction in life.

I left teacher training college with a teaching degree in Modern Languages, having pulled out all the stops during my final year. In terms of becoming a teacher, however, I hadn't shaken off my cynicism for the education system, which didn't bode well for the future.

~ 4 ~

Lost Opportunity

In the same way that my uncle got me a place at teacher training college, it was my sister-in-law who got me my first job. On the surface everything was falling nicely into place, with very little effort required on my part.

The position, teaching Modern Languages, was at Rannoch School in Perth and Kinross on the shores of the loch. The school, in the heart of the countryside, had been set up by four ex-Gordonstoun masters (the school which educated the Royal family), and the building itself was stunning, with the estate dating back to the middle-ages.

While I was pleased to have found work so easily, the feeling of discontentment at the back of my mind didn't go away… I longed for the city and some adventure, yet here I was, hiding away in the depths of the Scottish Highlands.

Rannoch School didn't have the highly academic reputation of Gordonstoun. The mornings were spent in traditional lessons, but the afternoons were given over to lots of activities, like sports, sailing and mountaineering. It was more like an outward-bound school than a traditional boarding school and, as such, attracted a lot of kids who didn't make the grade for Gordonstoun.

Wealthy wayward kids from Europe were sent to this God-forsaken school in the wilds of Scotland. Sixteen-year-old boys were practically brought to tears as their suitcases were searched by myself and other masters. Whisky, beer and cigarettes were confiscated as these renegades resigned themselves to a Spartan, grey Scottish existence.

The teaching staff were generally old, staid, and stuck in their ways. Being straight out of college, I found that I had far more in common with the sixth form students than I did with any of the teachers. It was quite a rebellious time for us because Sue and I, along with another couple who were also young teachers, used to have parties with the 18-year-olds.

The boys encouraged me to start a clay-pigeon shooting club – something I knew absolutely nothing about. They provided the guns, the ammunition and the education on what to do and, in return, I provided the safe haven of my accommodation to crack open the confiscated booze while we 'cleaned the guns'.

On one occasion, one of the schoolmasters decided he would organise a marathon around Loch Rannoch. The loch is 22 miles in circumference and so it didn't take much to find detours to cover the extra 4.2 miles. There were five of us, and the only training we did was three trips to the local pub in Kinloch Rannoch village – five miles there and five miles back. I again surprised myself at my grit and determination.

Despite identifying as a flaky, lazy loser, I obtained the creditable time of three hours 30 minutes, and so the flower of self-worth blossomed once again.

Overall, I did grow to love the school. It was well-run and very disciplined, but I still always had the feeling that I wasn't doing what I was meant to be doing. I would seek out opportunities to escape, then back down as soon as the first obstacle presented itself.

I was very into football at this point, having played at college and in Pitlochry, so when I was offered a place on an FA football coaching course to gain my Football Association Coaching badge, I decided to sign up and see if this could be a route out of teaching.

What happened next is something I've come to see as a pivotal moment in my life, one that really highlights the extent to which I'd become a 'zigzag' person...

Two of the coaches at the course were from the American team, the Atlanta Chiefs. Having watched me play, they came up and said, 'You're a very good player. Have you thought about playing in America?'

They explained that 'soccer' was just starting to take off in the States and that, because I was so good, I could play professionally over there and at the same time get involved at grass roots level and teach the kids in school.

It was a big opportunity for me, both in terms of my career and financially – the salary they were offering was double what I earned at Rannoch. For the first time in my life, I felt as if I actually knew what I wanted to do.

When I was interviewed and offered the job in America as a professional player for the Atlanta Chiefs, I knew my moment had arrived.

And then it hadn't. Seven days before Sue and I were due to start our new lives in America, I was playing in a match where I dislocated my ankle and broke three bones in my foot. So that was it. Game over.

The build-up to us leaving had been an incredible time. We had just discovered that Sue was expecting our first child and we were so excited to be starting this new chapter in our lives. I had given up my job at Rannoch School and although Sue and I didn't have a house to sell – I'd followed in my father's footsteps and taken the house that came with the job – we had sold all our furniture in preparation for us leaving for America.

I underwent an operation on my foot in Newcastle while Sue stayed with her mother in Carlisle. Once I was discharged from hospital, I also moved in with my mother-in-law. With my ankle in plaster, hobbling about on crutches, I didn't have much choice in anything!

This was a whole new low, from which I had no idea how to recover.

~ 5 ~

The Same Old Story

Not only was I completely out of action, I was also living with my mother-in-law, with no income and a baby on the way. I had gone from exhilaration to despair within a matter of days.

Following my operation, we stayed with Sue's mother for around six months. My first priority, as soon as I became more mobile, was to find myself a job. Naturally, I took the easy way out – teaching. It never entered my head to re-train for a different football team or even to reapply when my ankle healed, I simply zigzagged backed to familiar, safe territory.

Once again, my uncle came to the rescue, this time inviting us to stay with him while I looked for work, then driving me to my various job interviews because I was still in plaster at that time and walking with crutches. I had a total of four interviews around Matlock, one of which was at the celebrated Wells Cathedral School, before securing a position at Wrekin College in Shropshire.

Our son, Christopher, was born on 31st December 1982. Five days later, off I went to Wrekin College where a nice big house was waiting for us, just as there had been at Rannoch – and just as there always had been for my father. I put the whole idea of football to the back of my mind, filing it under 'not meant to be', and gave up on any thoughts of living in the US.

After the discipline of Rannoch School, I found Wrekin School far too liberal, with many of the teachers struggling to take control. The kids were all very well-off and some had a real air of entitlement about them, which grated on me.

My lack of both wealth and general success in life was truly rammed home to me on Leavers' Day at the end of term. Parents would arrive at the school in cars owned by their sixth-form offspring so the children could drive home. These cars were all brand new BMWs, Audis and Porsches; all newer and more luxurious than my car, or indeed any car belonging to a teacher at Wrekin College. This truly got under my skin.

Now that my big 'American dream' had been crushed, I hated everything about my new job: the school; the kids; the other teachers; and the whole area.

I managed to stay at Wrekin for 18 months, before moving further south and taking up a new position at Highfield School, a prep school in Liphook. I had no strategic plan in mind at that time, all I knew was that I had to get out of Wrekin.

~ 6 ~

Flying High

We moved to Liphook where I took up the new teaching post at Highfield School. To earn some extra money, I also started working as a commission-only salesman for the Porchester Group of insurance brokers in London. I used to commute from Hazlemere, taking the train into the City on my days off and during the school holidays.

The sales job didn't require any qualifications, just the ability to use the phone and read a cold-calling script! As the salary was solely commission-based, some members of the sales team were hugely successful, earning thousands of pounds a month, while others were barely able to afford the train fare home. It was dog-eat-dog, which was a completely new working environment for me and, whilst I soon realised that I didn't want to work like this forever, I saw an entirely new way of earning money. Suffice to say, working in a big commercial organisation was a real eye-opener for me.

There were 900 people in the offices which were big, plush and showy, right in the heart of the West End. I discovered that I really enjoyed the buzz of working in a team. It was a baptism of fire – going from teacher to salesman – but I thrived on it. The head of the sales department at Porchester was very keen for me to go full-time, but at that stage I needed the safety net of my fixed salary from teaching.

By the time I left the Porchester group, I knew I wanted a job with the kind of excitement I'd experienced in selling. I was really driven by the energy of commercial business and I was good at sales.

A new way forward had now opened to me and, following a brief spell of trying unsuccessfully to run a franchise business, I applied for various sales positions and was offered a job with a printing company called Surrey Printing. At last, I had a sense of my life starting to move in the right direction.

I left Highfield School and Sue and I bought our first flat. I now had a job I really wanted, and had bought my own home. Everything was taking off, and I was really starting to fly!

Only with hindsight did I realise that I was overriding my family patterns by buying my first property – my parents never owned a house.

Within the first year of working for Surrey Printing, I became their top salesman. This was exactly the validation I'd been looking for; the proof, if only for myself, that I was capable – more than capable – of moving into a job I really wanted and being successful at it.

I was no longer frozen by a fear of failure. This time, I was doing what *I* wanted to do, not blindly doing what was expected of me by others, however well-meaning. My problem, up until then, had been that I never valued anything highly enough, because I never had to work for it. Consequently, nothing mattered enough. I had spent so much of my early adulthood with a gnawing unhappiness, believing that whenever I tried to change anything, life pulled the shutters down on me. But it wasn't life blocking the way forward, as I believed at the time, it was me.

I went from strength to strength at Surrey Printing and attained the top salesman award. Money-wise, I had gone from barely scraping together £1,000 a month, to earning around £6,000 to £8,000 a month. It was at this point that I was approached by Derek, the Sales Director who had originally interviewed me for the position, asking me to meet him for a drink in the local pub one evening after work.

Derek told me that he was breaking away from Surrey Printing to set up on his own and was looking for two people to join him; he had the technical guy he wanted, and was now inviting me to join him as the Sales Director.

I didn't have to think twice, and said yes straight away. Derek and I had always got on very well and I knew we could make a success of things, which we did. Together, we started a company in Guildford called Zap Reprographics Limited, which was to become so successful that we attained the accolade of 'Digital Print Business of the Year' in 2006.

I'd finally become a straight-liner and had begun to understand that I could overcome all the obstacles of the past.

Nobody needs to live in the belief that their past life equals their future life. Everybody can reset their lives by overriding all that they've seen in family patterns and create the life they wish to lead.

~ 7 ~

Self-Help Junkie

I like to think that we all have golden moments in our lives and, for me, running my own business and living in a lovely house in the New Forest surrounded by my family, was exactly that; I was enjoying the life of a successful person. Meanwhile, Zap Reprographics went from strength to strength in terms of profitability and soon became a seven-figure company.

However, after 10 happy and successful years in business, dark clouds were gathering. This time, though, I had the resources to weather the storm and knew that to push through I had to take responsibility, not loiter hopelessly in the shadows hoping someone else would lead the way.

Things started to unravel. It was almost as if we had been riding on the crest of a wave for a decade, and now we were on the way down. Derek, who was not just my partner at Zap, but the person who'd been my mentor and guide in the printing business, began to lose his way. By now he was in his early 50s (I was in my 40s) and his focus was turning away from growing the company and towards getting out and taking early retirement.

His disillusionment projected into the core of the business, and I found myself working even harder, this time to fill the myriad gaps that were starting to appear. I've since learned that bad things start to filter from the top down in a business, and the discord between Derek and I affected most aspects of our company.

In monetary terms we continued to be successful. We had the management and staff in place to ensure we were not needed for the day to day running of the business, and had secured long-term contracts with large pharmaceutical giants and global corporates, like Coca-Cola, Nokia and Ericsson, as well as several big oil companies.

This time money wasn't the issue, however peace of mind and self-fulfilment were lacking in my life, so I started looking around for some answers; something to help set me on the path back to positivity and the life I wanted.

At around this time, I came across self-help coach Dan Millman. As well as running highly motivational courses, Dan wrote a book called *The Way of the Peaceful Warrior*, which I found inspiring to the point that I spent time in California, learning from Dan and attending his courses.

Dan taught that our arena for growth and learning is daily life, and that we are surrounded by lessons that will benefit us, provided we develop the awareness to wake up to them. I loved his relaxed approach and his quiet humour. He would liberally sprinkle trinkets of wisdom into his talks, then induce belly laughs from the audience with his sharp wit.

'Breathe, relax and look good' were repeated mantras he wished us to consider. Dan Millman woke me up to the belief that I need not live my life in fear – nor should any human being.

So began my quest to dilute and weaken the fears, doubts, and worries I had genetically inherited, as well as those imposed on me by negative influences and events.

I returned home energised, and raring to make changes in my life.

Back at work after attending a course in the US, the first thing Derek said to me was, 'Well, which weird practices have you brought back from *this* trip?' He asked a few questions about the sessions, and I told him some of what I'd learnt.

Once again he was cynical and suggested that Dan Millman's groups listened to his teachings, then went out in the world, automaton-like, doing exactly as we were told. This, from a man whose wife had, in recent years, corralled him into a Christian group who recruited new members on a network marketing basis, and who had recently returned from a weekend retreat where he had learnt how to 'speak in tongues'.

What had begun as a slight parting of the ways between me and Derek was rapidly becoming a huge chasm as we retreated to our separate corners, licking our wounds. Working with this man was becoming a living hell and, were a client of mine to have been in the same situation, I'd have said, *Get out – and get out quickly.*

However… I argued with myself that I had a loyalty to my staff to my clients, and in my better moods I reminded myself that I was grateful Derek had approached me to start this business.

We had been like peas in a pod for the first 10 years and, as the elder statesman, he had undoubtedly helped me develop both as a businessman and as a man.

However, whilst I had been growing in confidence, ability and fearlessness, like a young ambitious buck, Derek had begun retiring into a decline. For the past three years he'd been turning up to work at eight o'clock every morning, then spending the whole day practically slumped over his Bible until he left the office at five.

Nobody knew what he was actually working on during this period, and he would also regularly implore me to 'find something' for him to do. The business ran without him and the staff breathed sighs of relief when he was out of the office for a golf day.

Nevertheless, the business continued to thrive whilst he and I avoided one another as much as possible and our relationship limped along.

I was ready for my next challenge and, as they say, 'When the student is ready, the teacher appears.'

* * *

The consumption of self-help courses became my next phase as I threw myself into Reiki, martial arts, Neuro-Linguistic Programming (NLP), Emotional Freedom Technique (EFT) and too many others to mention. I became a personal growth junkie – some of it was great, some of it hilarious, and some of it downright crazy.

I recall my children bringing some friends from school round to our house for tea one afternoon. The guests timidly asked what the 'thump, thump' noise was coming from the side of the house. I think it was my daughter who nonchalantly answered that it was dad bashing his head against the wall! This was a new form of Hard Qi Gong I had studied, whereby one hardened all parts of the body so that you could be hit without being hurt. I was literally hitting the top of my head against the brick wall to strengthen it.

I was open to anything and everything, so when a business leader at a London meeting finished his workshop by saying '… but if you want *real* change in your life, phone Vikki in Denver, Colorado,' that's exactly what I did.

Vikki Faudel of the Mindset Team was, and is, a remarkable lady. Personal growth courses, together with my own self-awareness and actions, might have changed my life and my identity 100-fold, but I cannot put a value on Vikki's work with me. It was priceless, and I am eternally grateful that she came into my life.

Vikki created a method of working on the prefrontal cortex of the brain so that patterns of behaviour which don't serve us can be removed and replaced with positive empowering beliefs (discussed in more detail in chapter 12). She devised this system in collaboration with a neuroscientist and a chiropractor, whilst her intuitive, spiritual wisdom complemented this triumvirate of change-makers.

After removing further layers of the metaphorical onion, and stepping into the power of the man I had always believed was inside of me, I began to have clarity about where I was headed and what I wanted to do. Instead of being reactive and simply going along with whatever came my way, I developed the confidence to shape my life in exactly the way I wanted.

For several years I travelled to Vikki's home in Colorado, where she trained me in her methods so that I could pay forward all the amazing work she had done with me.

It was on one of these trips that I met Reg, a multi-millionaire businessman. At the zenith of his entrepreneurial career, Reg had a line of credit with the banks to the value of

100 million euros – that's how large his business became. Not wanting to miss the chance to quiz such a successful man, I asked the question on everybody's lips: 'What do you think is the basis of your incredible success?'

Without any hesitation he replied, 'I've always believed that whatever I wanted, I would get – and I always have.'

These simple words struck my brain like a bolt of lightning. My parents never believed they could get what they wanted. 'He who wants, never gets,' was a common refrain in my family.

In that moment I realized that this destructive belief is the reason so many people live lives of quiet desperation. It stirred a resolve in me to help and support as many people as I could to overcome this.

By many people's standards I was a success at this point in my life, but I still felt like much of what I did was reactive, initiated by others. It was now time to do exactly what I wanted and ensure that every day was proactively the best I could make it. I knew that if I could do this for myself, then I could inspire others to overcome their fears, doubts, and worries, allowing them to live their lives to the full.

~ 8 ~

The Month That Changed My Life

February 2008 was a pivotal month in the life of Geoff Sober. They say bad things come in threes, and three massive challenges were set before me to test my progress. The shit was about to hit the fan and I was about to learn, the hard way, whether my period of self-help awareness and mentoring had given me the resources to cope: Had my identity changed? Had I become more resilient to life's demands? Could I overcome fear when it came up close and personal? I was about to find out...

The first thing that happened was that my father passed away. No matter how much the loss of a parent hurts,

I'm certain that many of you who have experienced this would agree that the actual death is not the torment. The pain and suffering some humans experience as the precursor to death is excruciating and, as the caring observer of such suffering, it is a living hell to watch someone you love so dearly go through so much hurt.

My brother Gary who lived nearest to my parents in the northeast took most of the responsibility for ferrying my mother to see my father in hospital. As well as making visits himself, he did everything he could to reduce my parents' anxiety. I think it was clear to all who were close to my father that he simply wanted his suffering to end and pass into the next world.

In my family and business life, I have always tried to fix problems where I could and so I racked my brain as to what might be holding my father back from simply letting go. I could also sense my mother's despair. She had, in the main, accepted that he was slipping away and wished, for his sake, that he could be released from his torment.

I consulted Vikki Faudel, whose sixth sense could accurately read situations in a very different way. Her vision of events was that my father, worried about leaving my mother behind, was clasping onto this life, despite all the pain summoning him to the other side, because he didn't feel safe leaving her behind to cope.

In our traditionally northeastern family set-up, my father had always dealt with the finances – the house issues, the car, and all the general life admin to which my mother had never been a party – and this was what was keeping him in pain. Vikki suggested that when I was alone in the hospital ward with my father, I tell him that he must not concern himself about my mother and that I and my two brothers, Gary and Richard, would ensure she was looked after; that we would take his role and he need not remain in pain. Shortly after saying these words to my father, he passed away. Something deep inside tells me that was what he needed to hear in order to let go.

My father's passing did not weaken me and I gave the eulogy at his funeral, consoling those around me who were upset.

Life was demonstrating my metamorphosis from weak, fearful child to empowered human being – something we all have the ability to attain.

* * *

Whilst I was making 10-hour round trips up to Newcastle and back to visit my father in hospital and to comfort my mother and brothers, my second challenge was being caught up in buying Derek out of the print business (more about this in chapter 11).

This had been a tortuous process and the details are too long and arduous to describe here, but the long and short of it is that on the back of all the issues I was having with

Derek, I had taken the decision buy him out of the company, offering him the full valuation of the company in one hit, rather than negotiate a 'part now, part later' deal. This had become a finance-raising nightmare and an accounting conjuring trick.

The relationship between me and Derek had really soured by this time because, rather than accepting the buy-out valuation he was to have received 'all in one go', he had started asking for a salary for himself over the coming three years. He then asked that his wife be kept on in the position of credit controller. His demands kept on increasing; abusers like to control everything, and never tire of making more and more demands.

I received the news that my father had died on the day of a pre-arranged meeting to decide if Derek was going to get the 'extras' he was fighting so strongly for. I was able to remain calm, empowered and totally capable of dealing with my nemesis. I didn't postpone the meeting and, because I didn't want sympathy or emotion to enter a business transaction, I didn't tell Derek (or anyone else in the business) that I had just lost my father.

I was totally emotionless as I entered Derek's office and stated that there were to be no extras. He wasn't getting a 'consultancy' salary for the next three years and, while his wife could be considered for the credit control job, she would be interviewed and, if successful, would not be paid the high salary she had previously enjoyed.

Derek flew into a tantrum and shouted, 'After all I've done for you!' before kicking his chair towards me in an act of defiance.

I remained resolute and in control whereupon (as many bullies do) he turned to face the window, unable to look me in the eye, and started sobbing. 'Ok, if that's how it's going to be, then I have no other choice but to accept,' he said.

'Great I'll put this agreement in motion,' I replied. I turned to exit and then, on leaving added, 'By the way, my father died this morning so I'm going up to Newcastle to make the funeral arrangements. I'll be away for a few days.'

On that day I slayed not only the dragon that was my nemesis, but the dragon that embodied the fears I had carried with me for so much of my life.

* * *

'Never Rent a Room to an Armed Gunman' is the title of a talk I give to property investors. My third trial of February 2008 came in the form of an armed gunman. By this time, I had diversified my business interests and used some of my profits from the printing company to buy houses in Winchester.

The houses I own are all HMOs, or houses of multiple occupancy, that is houses rented out by the room, rather than as a whole, making them more profitable.

One prospective tenant I interviewed was a very pleasant young woman, whom I thought would fit perfectly with the other tenants, who were all female student nurses. As I handed over the keys, she politely asked whether it would be alright for her boyfriend to stay over from time to time. 'Sure,' I replied. There didn't seem to be any reason to refuse.

Unbeknown to me, the 'boyfriend' was awaiting a court date for armed robbery… and there was worse to come – he was also a known drug-dealer in the area. The couple began sharing the room together, then stopped paying rent. Two vicious Staffordshire bull terriers then appeared in the garden to protect this drug-dealing couple, and I began getting complaints from the other tenants that someone was rattling their doorhandles at night, presumably trying to get in.

The last straw came when some 'gangsters' from London turned up chasing a drug debt and kicked in the front door to try and get at him. Unfortunately, he must have been forewarned about this visit and so avoided a beating which might have persuaded him to move out.

When I rang the local police asking for advice on what to do about this situation, they were very pleased to hear from me. 'Oh, so that's where he is! Just keep him there so we know where he is as we've been trying to locate him,' I was told. How reassuring for myself and the other tenants in the house that at least the police knew where he was!

I decided to be proactive and, ignoring all the normal channels for eviction, I wrote the tenants a note telling them that as they hadn't paid their rent, I now wanted them out. I told them that I would be there at 2 pm the following Thursday, at which time they needed to be packed up and ready to leave.

Whilst I knew it wouldn't be as easy as that, I recognised that they would be expecting me to run scared of them, so I planned to confront them, demonstrating that I would not rest until they were out of the building.

On the day, I drove to Winchester and parked up near the house. I noticed there were four aggressive-looking men standing on each corner of the street. They had come prepared to do battle with a show of force, no doubt intended to persuade me to turn tail and run. I checked myself and knew that it was my destiny to face this evil, because that is exactly what these people embodied.

This all sounds very dramatic, yet the confrontation was largely uneventful. In my head I actually wasn't afraid. Something told me that I needed to go through with this, even if it turned out to be a violent encounter. More proof of who I had become; no more was I the fearful, reactive person hoping someone else would take away the problem. I was prepared to do whatever was necessary to overcome this evil.

The young woman did all the talking whilst the armed gunman stood behind her saying very little but hoping to intimidate me.

In the same way as my confrontation with Derek, I found I had a strength I hadn't previously known existed within me. I was calm, relaxed and resolute. I could tell that this man was picking up on my lack of fear as I moved closer to him and into his space, rather than away from him. Without any actual threats or angry words, I was able to communicate that he had no power over me. He started to ask if I had any odd jobs around the house he could do in lieu of rent, and with that I knew he was relenting and backing away from conflict. I told him no and explained that I would be starting the legal process to have them removed from the house and that in the meantime they should be looking for their next place to stay.

Yes, I had been practising martial arts for many years, but fighting in a dojo with degrees of respectability and discipline is quite different from fighting someone who has already proved themselves capable of pulling a gun to stamp their authority on a situation.

The young woman gave me a sob story about having had children taken off her and placed in care, of being abused herself as a child, and of then being in abusive relationships. She begged me to allow them to stay for the rest of the month. At this point the man's demeanour softened and he asked for sympathy for her because of her hard life. He had gone from trying to intimidate me to asking for my support.

Again, my experience of coaching and working with people helped me to see with clear eyes who and what these people were. I wasn't going to get them out that day, but I had confronted them, shown I wasn't afraid of any threat they wished to pose, and given them the ultimatum of leaving by the end of the month.

Using what I'd learned from personal growth work and martial arts, I took back the control they had taken from me when they stopped paying rent and put four hooligans on the street corners.

All three of these issues occurred simultaneously. If just one had occurred in my early life, it would have been enough for me to lose my mind, freak out and live every second of every day in fear. I truly believe these challenges were providence's way of saying to me, in no uncertain terms: 'Geoff, you are powerful beyond your wildest imagination. Go out and do exactly what you've dreamed of doing as you are invincible. You can deal with any problem life throws at you.'

In having all these new values instilled in my psyche, I could now trust life, and I could trust myself. I felt at peace with life. Instead of thinking life's events were out to get me, I'd had the lightbulb realization that life was working FOR me as, in truth, it always had been.

Let me repeat that – when you can see that life is working FOR you, then you relax into the flow of life and conquer your fears.

In summary, through handling all three above scenarios in an empowered manner, I was able to break their hold over me. I stepped up to the mark and the world didn't end. Instead, the following happened:

My brothers and I *did* look after our mother until her death, and actually she lived quite a fulfilled life in her 10 remaining years before passing herself.

I bought Derek out and took an 80% shareholding in the printing business. Escaping his clutches was truly liberating, and this experience has helped me support others in abusive relationships with controlling partners.

The armed gunman and his girlfriend didn't move out in one month, but one day I caught them on a 'low', when they hadn't enough money to buy drugs and were evidently hurting as a result, and I was able to pay them to leave the house. When I entered the room, I found it was full of stolen goods. There was an array of books about serial killers and evil, which was evidently his bedside reading. All the belongings they planned on taking to their next property were lined up, and he laughed as he held up his 'prison trousers' as proof of his past criminal record.

On inspecting the mess that was left behind, my cleaners and I counted 22 knives strategically placed in what was not a very big double room. This man might have had the capacity to dish out violence and fear, but he also lived in fear of the same being meted out to him and his partner. Vikki Faudel summarised this episode in these terms: 'You stood toe-to-toe with the devil and you won.' And that's exactly how it felt.

~ 9 ~

Becoming a Life Coach

The reason I became a life coach is simple – I've been there. So much of our unhappiness and lack of fulfilment comes from being trapped in the wrong life, too afraid to make those necessary changes. It's so easy to become stuck in a job you hate because you need the money, or stay in an abusive relationship because you are afraid of upsetting your abuser. When the journey to where you want to be in life seems scary, long and complicated, doing nothing is the easy option.

I was always dubbed a 'sensitive child' and was quick to show my feelings as a boy – not really the 'done thing' in a male-dominated northeastern family upbringing. I therefore changed this perception while still a child, realising that it worked against me. I now see that this very sensitivity was, and is, a gift, and far from being a vulnerability, it's a strength. It has helped me to get under the skin of my clients' worries and 'feel' their pain as if it were my own (the very inherited sensitivity which lost my mother her career as a nurse).

On the other hand, Vikki Faudel's training and the harsh reality of the life events I'd experienced gave me a protective toughness, which meant I could empathise with my clients' woes without making them my own, thus providing a better and more complete safety net.

At this point I could see life's plan – everything that had gone before was preparing me to serve my community. Every course I'd attended, every book I'd read, and all the events and people who had come in and out of my life, had brought me to this moment. It felt like my innate talents, which I had denied for so long, had an outlet. If every human being has their own personal innate skills, then it was my role to help them express these and feel emboldened by this newfound self-worth.

I have been so lucky to have experienced the worlds of education, sport, business, sales, coaching and mentoring, speaking and writing, property management and investing, and in doing so have encountered many of the barriers to happiness and fulfilment which plague others' lives.

I can now see that the years I spent alone in the countryside were my years for reflecting and thinking, without the usual teenage distractions to divert me from looking inwards.

I started very young on the self-improvement trail and recall using my father's Bullworker, a new-fangled workout tool for building muscle. At age 12, I bought myself a barbell and a set of weights – even at that early age, I was experimenting with how I could be 'better'.

My rebellion against education allowed me to pursue wisdom, rather than filling my mind with pointless facts and figures that I would never use or need. I also came to understand why I hadn't fitted in with so many of the teachers I worked alongside. Having attained their university degrees, it seemed they considered themselves 'the finished article' and stopped learning. Too many of these academics, with their tunnel vision, revelled in the idea that a degree in a specialised subject was the mark of a superior human being. In the same vein, I witnessed far too much vanity within the schools where I taught, with scant humility and little thirst for further learning.

Whilst I met some amazing and wonderful educators for whom I have nothing but praise and admiration, I also encountered many who, like me, had gone into teaching simply because they didn't know what they were good at and were too afraid to steer themselves away from the educational system, where they felt comfortable.

It was Vikki Faudel who first told me that I should coach and mentor others – something I'll discuss in more detail later on – to which my first reaction was a form of imposter syndrome: 'Nobody wants to be coached!' I exclaimed. None of us do, of course, we simply want to decide on our path in life, follow it, and hope that our journey is fulfilling and makes us money. However, it's not always that simple. Many people just don't know what they want from life, or, if they do know what they want, then often they are afraid to go and get it.

I protested further with Vikki, saying, 'But surely everything I know about personal growth and how to live a happier, wealthier, healthier life is already out there?' Indeed, there are libraries full of the wisdom I would be teaching, not to mention gurus aplenty spreading the word on how to live a better life.

'Yes, but some people will only hear what they need to hear from you,' Vikki wisely replied.

I've included this point in particular for anyone reading this who doubts themselves. Yes, there will be many people doing what you intend to do, but you are unique, with a special part to play on this earth, imprinting your gift on others.

Indeed, I now see that Vikki was right and that there's a distinct connection between me and the clients I attract. I believe that our paths collided for a reason, borne out in the fact that nearly all of my clients have become my friends, having mutually benefited one another.

Above: William Murray, the Grand Master

Below: The Murray residence in Gateshead

My parents, Arthur and Dorothy

Centre front – wearing a brown suit to prove I'm not a pupil

Above: Rannoch School - 1980

Below: Wrekin College, Academic Staff - 1983

Back row second person in on the right

73

Me in vest and white shorts

Above: My one and only marathon around Loch Rannoch

Below: Article in the Cumberland News
following my footballing injury

Above and below: With my wife, Sue

PART 2

~ 10 ~

Silencing Your Inner Critic

One of the fundamental barriers to achieving what we want in life is listening to criticism, most of which comes from within. In other words, We are our own worst critic. The story we tell ourselves is: That's going to be scary; I won't do that. So we don't. We don't start up a conversation with that person we'd like to get to know because we think they won't be interested; we don't go to the gym because we tell ourselves we're too out of shape; we don't start a business because we believe we don't have enough experience and think we are bound to fail.

But where does the inner critic come from? It often starts early, which was certainly true in my case...

Growing up in Gateshead, I was the eldest child in an extended family with grandparents, great-grandparents, aunts and uncles all living nearby – and they would all gossip. My mother, for example, would let it be known when I was suffering from some childhood ailment, such as the eczema or asthma to which I was prone, and then listen to all the various pieces of advice, most of which were thinly veiled criticisms: *Oh, you treated Geoff with that? That's not a good idea, I would have done it like this…*

My mother felt judged at every turn, then turned that judgement on me. Nothing I did was ever quite right, or done the way she thought it should have been done. Eventually, the voice of criticism rang loudly in my ears: *You did that quite well, but not perfectly.*

The inner critic stands at the gateway to perfectionism waiting for us to pass through… and once we enter the realms of perfectionism, it becomes almost impossible to take action. My mother was fearful in so many areas of her life; a pattern of behaviour she learned from her own parents.

As a child and as a young adult, my mother lived in the shadow of her brother, who was praised for his brilliant academic achievements and skill as a musician. My mother, on the other hand, was continually criticised, judged, and blamed. Her parents' expectations of her, that she would simply marry and become a housewife, were so low that a sense of failure would have been instilled in her from the outset, which she then passed down to me and my brothers.

The inner critic can begin at home, or at school, where we might be told by a teacher that we're doing something wrong, or rather, that we're not doing it 'by the book' or according to the rules. When a young child is hauled up before the class and told off for making a mistake or, worse still, mocked, the door is opened wide for the inner critic to take up residence and settle in for the duration. Of course, this doesn't happen in every case, only to those children with a vulnerability. A different child might breeze through school and early life, especially if they have a sympathetic parent giving encouragement and telling them not to worry. However, for those who do possess that vulnerability, the inner critic becomes part of their identity, staying with them for life, unless it can be silenced.

In my case, there are many instances of the inner critic speaking to me from a young age. One particular example I remember happened at primary school. We used to be taken swimming every Friday and the first award we had to pass was the 25-yard badge. Week after week I just couldn't get there. I'd heard my mother talk about my asthma so many times, that I decided I was a lousy swimmer because I couldn't get my breath, which was never going to improve. The fact that I could run up and down the school field playing football perfectly well, or go cross-country running, never occurred to me.

When I finally swam those 25 yards, the whole class stood watching at the side of the pool and clapped when I got to the end. I didn't experience any feelings of pride or elation, I just felt like I was the odd one out. Everyone else had managed it easily, except me. I wasn't good enough. I was the class failure.

Except I wasn't a 'failure', I had just been listening to my inner critic – who was a liar. The truth of the matter was that all my family hated swimming and while other parents took their children to the pool or for lessons, mine never did. It was my father, in particular, who wouldn't go near water. His introduction to swimming lessons happened during his National Service, and he would tell the story of all the swimmers being lined up on one side of the pool and all the non-swimmers on the other side. The non-swimmers were then pushed into the water and left to fend for themselves, so you can only imagine his fear. He never got over it and throughout his life hated anything to do with the water, even going in a boat.

As an adult, I can now re-frame my experience of the swimming lessons. I wasn't a failure, I had simply never been taught to swim. How could I, when I'd never even visited a swimming pool?! My mind had been filled with the negative reinforcement that water was bad and swimming was dangerous, which wasn't my fault. I'd been following a pattern of negative behaviour that I had learned – which meant I could unlearn it.

I had a client with a similar issue of a negative pattern learned when she was very young, which, over the years, had morphed into a fear of public speaking. The client in question traced her fear back to an incident at school when she was asked to read aloud by the teacher and pronounced the word 'ambulance' wrong. The whole class laughed at her and the humiliation of that day stayed with her into adulthood, making her introverted as a teenager, despite her having been quite an outgoing child.

With my help, she was able to re-frame that past experience of humiliation. We discussed viewing the incident through adult eyes. 'You were a child back then,' I told her. 'The feelings you had then were the feelings of a child which were perfectly understandable at the time, but you have to stop blaming yourself. You know how to pronounce "ambulance" now.'

Following our sessions, she was able to draw a line in the sand under that traumatic childhood event. She didn't need hours of therapy and analysis, just the awareness that one incident in her past had magnified, transforming itself into her adult inner critic. It was time to understand that voice for the lie that it was, then let it go.

From a personal point of view, I know that I inherited my father's fear of failure. A further example of this was his turning down a potential 'offer of a lifetime' on being discharged from his National Service.

My father had been singled out as a very skilled football player by his sergeant (also a very good player) who told him: 'I've organised two trials for you. One of them is with a first division club and one is with a third division club. Turn up at these trials and do what you do. I think you can make it as a professional footballer.'

Needless to say, my father never turned up for either trial. That to me, was classic fear of failure. His inner critic told him he wasn't good enough so, in his mind, it was easier all round not to show up at all. That story really saddens me.

Part of what I now do with my coaching, is getting people to recognise that the negativity in their lives often comes directly from the inner critic. *Okay,* I say to them, *So what is that critic saying to you, and where did that voice originate from?*

This doesn't need to be a long, drawn-out process in terms of therapy. In fact, people generally cotton on to it straightaway. For me, the realisation that the inner critic was feeding my fear of failure came during what I've termed as my spell of being a 'personal growth junkie', when I was going from seminar to seminar feeling motivated initially, but then finding nothing actually changed for me. You could say I'd become a circle person. *It's alright for you up there on stage, I would think, but you don't know what it's like being me right now.*

Off I would go to one of Dan Millman's courses in California, where I'd walk on coals or do a bungee jump, only to come home to the same old scenarios and find myself stuck again.

In addition to Dan Millman, I also listened to a personal growth guru called Tony Robbins, who is a very well-known life-coach. This guy is a six-foot, seven-inches tall American giant with a gravelly voice who commands a huge presence on stage. He is a billionaire who owns an island, as well as countless businesses, and has amassed a huge following. I used to feel incredibly motivated watching him speak, but at the same time the voice inside my head would be saying, *I can't be like that. I'm not six feet seven with a huge smile and all that charisma...*

Now I understand that my inner critic was just putting up a stop sign saying, *If you can't be like Tony Robbins, then why even try? Stay small; it said. Stay with who you are now – it's hopeless trying to be like Tony Robbins.*

Many people who aren't living the lives they want might look for, and find, inspiration in seminars and self-help books. At the same time, however, the inner critic is saying *That won't work for you. You're not like that.* Doubt, worry and fear of failure are all swirling together in this melting pot within the mind and from this comes the feeling of, *I can't. I can't start that business, get that job, or achieve that goal.*

I've said that one of my key breakthrough moments was understanding that my inner critic had been formed in childhood, and that it was largely the voice of my parents' fear. At this point, I should add that a lot of their negativity also came from their efforts to protect me when I was young. A child is told, *Don't touch the stove, or you'll get hurt,* but as they grow older, that can spill into the realms of over-protectiveness and the message becomes, *You're a child, you're not able to look after yourself. You need someone to protect you and stop you doing anything that might be harmful.*

In order to help silence the inner critic, I advise my clients to start a journal. This really helped me detach myself from *my* inner critic. For example, if I'd been asked to give a talk on stage and had then started to think, *I can't do this speech,* or *I'm not good enough, no one will listen to me,* I would write down what I wanted to achieve in my journal, clearly setting out my goals, then set the negative thoughts down on paper. This gave me awareness of what exactly it was that I wanted so that I could separate my goals from the negativity of the voice in my head.

    Looking at the words on the page, I was able to create the distance to ask myself, 'Where's the evidence that I can't do any of these things?' There was, of course, no evidence. The more I read over the doubts, the more diluted they became, losing their power to influence me.

    Writing down the words the inner critic is telling you exorcises them – they are outside of you, so you can view them in a cold, detached manner.

    There is a ploy used by hypnotists which runs like this:

Close your eyes and get quiet.

*Wait until the mind chatter starts and undoubtedly
the inner critic will kick in.
Isolate a critical voice and imagine it as a squeaking
mouse – pick it up by the tail and place it into a jam
jar.
Each critical voice is a squeaky mouse, so fill the jar
with the annoying 'mice'.
When you run out of voices, put the lid on the jar
and pretend there is a volume control on the jar
Turn it up really loud so that you can listen to the
guilt-mongering, angry, blame-inducing voices, then
turn it right down and keep it down so that you shut
out these imaginary critics who serve no useful
purpose in your life.
Your mind, or should I say your inner critic, tells you
lies and you have to call it out.*

Now, I laughed cynically at the concept of visualising
'squeaky mice', but this method (with our without squeaky
mice) has worked well with clients in relationships they had
perceived as permanent, thinking they had met the love of
their life, only to discover that the other person wanted to
leave.

The initial thoughts are always, *What's wrong with
me? Why wasn't I good enough?* If you keep these thoughts
in your head, you will breed self-loathing and shame;
however, by seeing them as 'squeaky mice' and dispensing

them to the jam jar, the injured party starts to see there is nothing wrong with them as a person and their partner making the choice to leave them does not imply any inadequacies on their part. Giving the inner critic a separate identity, like the squeaky mice, ensures we don't take on unnecessary self-blame.

This worked very well for one particular client of mine, and, when coaching her, I would say, 'This negative part of your mind is a liar and is not part of you. It's constantly telling you things that aren't true. What might you call this voice in your head to separate it from the rest of your thoughts?'

'Well…' she said, 'I had an old granny who used to always blame and criticise me, and I can most definitely identify my negative thoughts with her voice.'

I told her that was perfect, and so we named her inner critic 'old granny'. Now she will often tell me the things that 'old granny' has said to her, recognising that they are lies and that she doesn't have to listen to them.

There's a great deal of research out there about separating yourself from the inner critic. For example, the National Science Foundation reckons that we have anything between 12,000 and 60,000 thoughts per day and that a huge 80% of those thoughts are negative. Ninety-five per cent of that 80% are the same thoughts we had yesterday!

The message is clear, if you want change in your life, you have to change the thoughts circling in your head that are dictating who you are and how you should act. That's the trouble with listening to the inner critic – it's continually regurgitating the same old thoughts of self-blame, self-criticism and self-judgment.

As Albert Einstein cited: 'The thinking that got us to where we are, is not the thinking that will get us to where we want to be.'

Another case study of mine struggling with his inner critic is Nick, a highly intelligent chartered surveyor. Throughout his life, Nick had been associated with the property business in one way or another, even as a child helping his property-developer father.

Nick got a good degree before working nine-to-five for the council. His dream, however, had always been to create wealth via property investment and development, yet when it came to moving towards this goal, he was completely blocked.

Our paths crossed at a property seminar which I attended when building my own property business. Nick told me he had recently spent £15,000 on a property investing course, but just couldn't get started. It was hard to understand the reasons behind this, as it appeared that property was in his genes.

At that stage I had quite a substantial property portfolio myself, yet had barely a fraction of Nick's knowledge and experience. Nick, however, constantly talked about his lack of confidence and was paralysed into apathy through fear.

'Where is the evidence that you can't do this?' I would ask him. 'Because the fact is, you come from a background of knowing exactly what to do. You do it every day in your job. You project-manage buildings.'

To cut a long story short, I worked with Nick for a long time and although his was quite a challenging case, together we chipped away at his barriers and worked hard to silence that inner critic. Initially, he was reluctant to let go of his negativity, to the point that I would allow him 10 minutes at the start of each coaching call to get all his unfounded concerns off his chest, after which we would start looking at what he actually *could* achieve.

Nick would constantly ask himself, *Why am I like this? What's wrong with me?* Sometimes I would literally have to tell him that his negativity time was over and to just stop! He was very much a circle person when we first started working together, wallowing in his own personal quagmire of doom and gloom and thinking he would never get out of it. *What if I lose money? What if the house has subsidence? What if…?*

All his fears doubts and worries were focussed on the end result; the outcome. He needed to understand that his inner critic was taking him too far into the future, and that the only way to achieve his goal was to take things one step at a time.

'There are no facts to suggest that anything bad is

going to happen,' I would tell him. 'Stop listening to your head and let's make a plan to get your first project off the ground.'

Once we had silenced his inner critic (or at least turned down the volume), we could begin again. 'Now, let's assume you *are* going to take a step towards your goal, where shall we begin?' I would ask. I would then task him with 'homework' which involved taking just one step, like finding a suitable property on Rightmove, or considering where and how he might raise the finances. All 'just for the fun of it' to get the ball rolling. Breaking the process down into actionable steps focussed Nick's mind on what *was* possible, showing him that in as little as one week, he could make some very positive progress towards his goal.

Slowly but surely, Nick has been able to turn his life around and is now on the road to achieving his goal. As of writing, he has bought his first development project and is in the throes of re-building and renovating. By the end of July 2023, he should be depositing a nice fat 'six-figure profit' cheque into his account.

As an example, let's consider what would happen if we allowed the inner critic to take control of our attempts to pass a driving test. There are many people who don't pass their driving test first time, some even having second, third and fourth attempts… and beyond. And yet, because driving is so important in our lives, we don't think *Oh well, I failed that so there's no point in my trying again. I'm clearly just a failure,* which is exactly what we do in so many other aspects of our lives. We need that driving licence, so we take another test, and another, until we pass.

The driving test may be labelled a 'Fail' but that doesn't mean *we* are a 'Fail'.

As Zig Ziglar said, 'Failure is an *event*, not a person.'

In short, the inner critic is always fast-forwarding to the end goal, then giving us all the reasons we can't achieve it. That voice translates into fear of failure which, in turn, becomes an insurmountable barrier.

The key piece of advice to bear in mind when faced with fear of failure is this: ACTION TRUMPS THOUGHT. This is a recurring theme throughout my coaching. The only way forward is to stop zig-zagging and circling and become a 'straight-liner'. We don't need to over-analyse where our inner critic came from, we just need to recognise that it lies to us. The patterns we inherit from way back in our past are not our fault. We took them on, which means there's no reason why we can't shake them off.

> *Do you try and pick up a pencil? No, you just pick it up.*
> *Do you try and get a job? No, you just get a job.*
> *There is no 'try' there is only do or don't do*

.

~ 11 ~

Don't Be a People-Pleaser -
Stop Listening to the Doubters

The person who fears failure is often a people-pleaser; that is, someone who will do whatever it takes to win the approval of others.

I spent most of my early life being a people-pleaser. This meant that I took every opportunity to validate my status by putting other people's needs and wants before my own.

As a boy, birthday parties were less about me, and more about making sure all my guests were happy and doing what they wanted to do. If I wanted to play hide and seek but someone else asked to play musical chairs, then musical chairs it was. Over the years, these behaviours became ingrained and I learned the following:

I didn't matter.
I wasn't important.
My needs, wishes and desires were secondary.
My role was to serve and sacrifice.
Conflict and confrontation weren't worth the hassle.

I would do favours for anyone who asked me, yet never asked for one in return lest it put someone to any trouble.

This inherent need to please others started with my parents. I've already talked about my father working for the National Trust and his job bringing him into contact with a lot of landed gentry and members of the aristocracy, and this is where my life as a people-pleaser began. I was brought up with the idea that these people were 'above' us, because that's how my parents felt. I heard it in my mother's telephone voice to Lady Wendy Lycett, and in my father's need to be liked by everyone – that was his identity. He was a 'nice' man and we were a 'nice' family.

My parents lived their entire lives focussed on pleasing others. After my father passed away, my mother would receive many kindly offers of help from neighbours in her Northumberland village. It's what everybody did: 'Do you want something picked up from the shops, Dorothy?' she'd be asked, or a young lad would knock on the door saying, 'Would you like your lawn done?' When my mother asked how much it would cost, the answer was always, 'Oh no, nothing at all, it's a favour.'

Yet she couldn't accept this kindness: 'Here, take a tenner for your trouble,' she'd say, unable to accept anything for free, for fear of what people might think of her. That, to me, is the epitome of people-pleasing; the fear of owing a debt of gratitude, or being thought less of.

Taking the cue from my parents, I dutifully took on the role of people-pleaser for myself. As the eldest child, I tried particularly hard to please my mother. She was a fantastic cook, yet if she made anything I really didn't like, I'd eat it regardless just to please her. She often made a baked Alaska which I always ate – she never knew how much I hated it as I never said a word!

Needing to be loved, accepted and approved of is part of being human, but the people-pleaser takes this to a new level, being content to suffer misery and pain in the cause of letting another person get what they want.

Fearing rejection and criticism from my parents, in particular my mother, made me a people-pleaser and I put her needs, both emotional and physical, ahead of my own at every opportunity. Unfortunately, she was unable to give me the praise, support and unconditional love needed to offset this people-pleasing. Having never received that love and support from her own mother, she had no understanding of what was required.

The legacy of people-pleasing ran deep and, albeit unconsciously, my upper-most thought on meeting anyone was always that I should make them like me, and I did indeed become very likeable which, on the surface, appeared to validate my experience. If, despite my efforts, it became evident that somebody didn't like me, my world would come crashing down and I would try different approaches to win them over.

People-pleasers think they are being humble, but as the writer C. S. Lewis said, 'True humility is not thinking less of yourself, it is thinking of yourself less.' In being ultra-sensitive to how they are perceived by others, people-pleasers become immersed in projecting the 'right' image, turning all their thoughts inwards towards themselves.

People-pleasing is such a difficult trait to remove because the individual concerned becomes convinced that not pleasing others makes them a bad person. Having spent all their life up until that point receiving the affirmation that they are 'good', 'nice' and 'well thought of', a change to this perception of the self would invalidate their chosen identity.

In fact, this type of person is so lacking in self-worth and internal confidence that they constantly need top-ups of validation. Consequently, it becomes imperative that the butcher, the baker, and even the candlestick-maker, all think well of them. A people-pleaser will leave a restaurant tip commensurate not with the level of service they received, but in accordance with how they want to be perceived by the waiting staff, even if they are unlikely to ever visit that restaurant again.

An uncle of mine would go out of his way to crack jokes, ask questions and engage in 'interested' conversation with anyone and everyone from the service industries. We were once all at a family event with extended relatives in attendance, only to discover that, unfortunately, the accommodation in the designated hotel was abysmal; so much so, that my wife and daughter slept in their overcoats because they found pubic hair in the bed. To make matters even worse, there was mould growing in a crack in the bedroom sink and even remnants of blood on one of the walls. Finally, to cap it all, their door didn't lock. Nearly all the other rooms had similar horror stories. I duly complained to the owner, along with other members of the family, who in response held up his hands and bemoaned his lack of money, and thus his inability to make any improvements.

Whilst most of us were angry and upset at this shoddy treatment, there was my uncle chatting away blithely about how brave the owner was to take on a business like this. He sympathised with his lack of money, and I believe he even left a tip.

This was a people-pleaser extraordinaire. If it had been the playground, he would have cocked a snoot at the rest of us saying, 'The owner likes me more than he likes all of you!'

He had to validate himself by being liked. However, in this way he played the victim to this man as he paid full price, plus tip, whereas the rest of us received refunds because the owner knew his place wasn't fit for guests to stay there.

This was the moment I saw how wide and deep the need to please people ran within my family.

As I went through life, I could have become very conceited at the number of people who wanted to 'partner' with me: my German college tutor asked me to join him in the new school where he was to be head of Modern Languages; a singing teacher wanted me to partner with her in her business; and, of course, Derek asked me to partner with him in the digital print business.

It was only after I had worked on myself and cleared a lot of my inner garbage that I developed the clarity to see that I was the ideal partner because I was such a 'yes' man. Ask me to do it and it was done. Want me to agree with you? I'll agree. Want to feel good about yourself? Then I'll support you and tell you how great you are.

This is what I've witnessed amongst my coaching clients:

> *The man who sent so much money back to his family abroad that he barely ate, and yet they kept telling him it wasn't enough.*

The woman who had one child to try and make her partner love her and treat her well, and when that didn't work, she had a second child, and a third. He didn't change, and they are no longer together.

The builder who was always giving work away free of charge, or providing discounts because being liked was more important than being paid a fair rate for his work.

What many people-pleasers don't understand – and I didn't comprehend this myself until later in my life – is that when one individual is giving over their opinions, their values and their lives to another, it constitutes abuse.

It is extremely hard to be a success, or indeed to be at one with yourself and be happy, if you can't put yourself first on your priority list. This is not being selfish, arrogant or egocentric. You are allowed to want what you want in life, providing wanting that thing doesn't hurt anybody else.

My awakening to who I was and what was blocking my health, wealth, success and inner happiness came when I understood that I was working with a business partner whose behaviour towards me was abusive.

Abusers don't come with a big 'A' tattooed on their foreheads, and in truth, Derek came into my life at the perfect time. He was there when I needed 'saving' and was, in short, my rescuer. I believe that life gives you stages of growth and realisation, and my chance to play football in the US had been the stuff of dreams, with my believing that there was something better for me out there, something other than teaching.

When that all came crashing down, I looked around for another opportunity and thought I'd found the answer when I came across the chance to buy a Postal Centres franchise. I didn't have the £20,000 outlay to start the business, so I took out a loan from the franchisor's appointed lender.

Owning a Postal Centre franchise entailed selling portable display units to post offices and convenience stores, who in turn obtained income from local businesses placing advertisements on the display unit. I was given the wealthy Surrey area and while still teaching languages as a day job, I ventured out into the business world selling these units.

They were a tough sell, but with my 'people-pleasing' personality and my honest transparency, I made sales. However, one day when I phoned the head office for my commission, I found the phone line was out of service. I tried repeatedly, but still got the same message.

A couple of Sundays later, I opened *The Sunday Times* to see the franchise owner splashed across the pages! He had skipped the country with the Fraud Squad hot on his heels, having taken all the franchisees' money with him – and apparently not for the first time.

I was left with an outstanding debt of £20,000 for a business that now had no infra-structure (and therefore wasn't viable) with no way of paying it back. Naturally, I saw the whole episode as yet another failure and doubted my ability to ever run a business and make money.

As such, I was in quite a desperate state, both mentally and financially, when I applied for the job at Surrey Printing. It was Derek who took a chance on me when I had no real experience of selling, taking me under his wing and supporting me as I rose to become the top seller in the company. I got the company car, an expense account and an entertainment allowance. I'd been almost on the point of despair, but this job – and Derek – saved the day.

At first, Derek and I got along well. He was supportive and encouraging, which I really appreciated. A 'rough and ready' character, he would often brag about how well he done in life. 'Look where I've got to…' he was fond of telling anyone who would listen. 'Not bad for someone who grew up on a council estate.' He saw me as an academic and, as such, very different from him – I was 'book smart' while he was 'street smart'. I think he almost saw me as a challenge to be overcome.

Derek was very tough on me in those early days. Once, when I was late for a sales meeting, he called me out in front of the whole sales team and tore me off a strip, then made me go out at lunchtime and buy the whole team a box of Ferrero Rocher (I don't think one of those chocolates has ever passed my lips since). And he didn't stop there. When the 'Young Salesman of the Year' was about to be announced, the whole team looked towards me as my sales figures and performance made it a foregone conclusion, however, Derek chose to give it to someone else whom everyone knew had performed less well. He later explained this was down to my being late for that sales meeting.

At that stage I still believed Derek had my best interests at heart and that his way of showing tough love would push me on to greater things. Eventually he would single me out in sales meetings, using my sales record as an example. I was the archetypal 'blue-eyed boy' and the others must have hated me. *Geoff does it this way... Geoff does it that way... Why don't you do it like Geoff...?* he would say.

Consequently, I developed a strong loyalty towards Derek which I felt was returned; never more so when he asked me to meet him after work at the local pub that time. 'I'm sick of my co-directors enjoying all the spoils of our endeavours,' he confided. 'I think there is a niche we can fill, that isn't being addressed.'

Then came the crucial words: 'I'd like you to be my business partner.'

I had no hesitation. I'd reached the top in this company and was now much more my own person, confident and ready for a new challenge. I knew Derek was a strong character and that things would have to change if we were to sustain a business – rather than boss/employee – relationship.

However, at that stage my excitement at starting a new business outshone any underlying misgivings.

Anyone reading this who has started a business from scratch will understand that the first few years are a blur of activity. You simply live and breathe your business and don't have much head space to step back and analyse what is actually happening.

Realisations don't always happen in one flash of insight, sometimes small incidents which you label as 'strange' at the time, start to mount up until they are unveiled as truths. For me, that first small realisation about my business relationship with Derek (and who I was in that relationship) came about 18 months after we'd set up the business together.

At the start of our new venture there were three of us, as Derek also brought a highly skilled technical guy on board, Chris, who really was a print genius. It wasn't an equal three-way split, however. Derek had a 50% share of the business, while Chris and I had 25% each.

You could say that from the outset, Derek had set the scene with me and Chris as his subordinates, although at the time, I didn't see it that way. As far as I was concerned, I was doing well in my own right; I was making money; I was growing the business by bringing in large corporate clients; and I was enjoying learning more about how to grow a successful business.

Eighteen months later, Derek and I decided it was time

to let Chris go. Chris was, as I've said, a brilliant technician, however his attitude was predominantly negative. If a big print job came in after five o'clock in the evening, he would invariably have an excuse for not staying to see it through: football training, his pub night with the boys... He had plenty of excuses to skip off on time, while Derek and I worked through the night. His wasn't the approach of someone committed to running a successful business.

A package was put together to buy Chris out, but here's the interesting 'people-pleasing' part: Derek said to me, 'I'll take all Chris's shares,' and I accepted this. He never suggested I take any of Chris's shares for myself, and I never thought to ask.

It could have been an opportunity for me and Derek to have become equal partners, but the thought didn't cross my mind and it was never discussed. I thought, *If Derek says he's taking Chris's share, then that's what's happening,* it was as simple as that. Yet something didn't sit right with me.

You could say that Derek and I became victims of our own success. We had reached a point in the business whereby things were running profitably with minimal input from either of us. Then Derek began to change, both in his dealings with the business and in terms of his personality.

Firstly, he got bored with the company. 'Geoff, I've got nothing to do. Can you find me something to do?' he would   say.

Secondly, and as far as I was concerned more

destructively, he became part of an all-consuming religious movement. From this point onwards it became harder and harder to communicate with him.

A key warning sign that I had started to become Derek's victim was highlighted to me when we started a website division. The internet was starting to explode and, while every corporate organisation had sophisticated brochures in cyberspace, I could see that small and medium businesses were not waking up to the power of e-commerce, or even the basic benefits of selling their brand via a well-designed website.

With this in mind, I found a much-needed technical whizz kid whom we tested by asking him to design our website. He received plaudits from all corners and was willing to work with us on a freelance basis.

However, Derek at once overrode my decision on hiring the new website technician on a freelance basis, and suggested the guy gave up his day job and worked for us full time instead, offering him a lucrative salary and a company car. My vision for the unfolding of this new part of our business was completely discarded. It was as if I'd been handed the freedom to create something new, and then had it immediately taken back off me.

Again, I reiterate that a people-pleaser is someone who cares more about how another is feeling than himself. He or she submits; doesn't speak up; shrugs their shoulders and suffers frustration and demotivation.

The cracks in our relationship widened even further when Derek sat me down in his office and said, 'I've decided that we will build the website company up to a certain level and you can take your salary from there, which will make the print side look more profitable.'

This marked a significant turning point in my attitude towards Derek. In starting up the website business, I'd envisaged having a dual income stream that included my salary from the print side, but Derek clearly had other ideas.

It was becoming abundantly obvious that his personal agenda trumped everything else. He wanted to make the printing business appear as profitable as he could in order to maximise its value in time for him to sell it a few years down the line when he retired. Safeguarding *my future* and increasing *my* potential income stream didn't even enter his head.

I now began to rapidly lose interest in the business. The ties that had been slowly loosening were all but severed and I was consciously extracting myself from my need to please him. I had allowed Derek to take the reins at every opportunity, and in doing so I had slowly but surely lost my identity. He was in control and I had allowed it to happen by putting him on a pedestal. Now that the pedestal was crumbling beneath him, I was able to put a psychological distance between us.

At one point I approached him and said, 'Listen, why

don't I leave the business? I need to find something else now. If I leave the company, you can bring in a new salesperson at a lot less money than I'm taking out and I'll retain my shares.' But no, he wouldn't countenance that at all.

What happened next marked a significant step forward for me – I bought my first rental property. That was when I really broke away. I didn't tell Derek what I'd done, although it was the sort of thing we would have openly discussed in the past. We used to talk and share everything, but now it was clear that there was another agenda going on.

The point of this story is to demonstrate that my confrontation with Derek that day my father died – denying him all his wants and conditions and pushing back – marked a huge shift in my career as a people-pleaser. It was over. Derek hadn't allowed me to be myself.

As a people-pleaser, I had lost my identity, which is what happens. Furthermore, *I* had let it happen. With hindsight I think to myself, *Geoff, YOU should have taken responsibility,* but apportioning blame, be it one way or the other, isn't productive.

That episode in my life now stands as an example to myself – and to anyone reading this book – that I needed to stand up for myself and stop being a people-pleaser.

We are here on this earth to claim our space, to be happy and to be great – to be ourselves. We need to embrace our identity and be that person, not avoid it because we think everyone else is more important than us. People-pleasers stay trapped in this version of themselves, because they listen to the doubters; those who say, 'You're not the kind of person who can...' or 'You don't have the ability to...' People-pleasers then take this negativity on board and absorb it, content to maintain the status quo rather than turn round and confront someone, saying 'You're wrong, I can....' or, 'I am that sort of person...'

As an example, a young female client of mine started dating a new boyfriend whom she thought was going to be her partner for life. As a people-pleaser, she gave herself over to him completely and started taking an interest in motor racing, rugby and anything else that interested him. She gave up the things she enjoyed doing and threw herself solely into his hobbies.

An abuser loves a people-pleaser as they can take complete control of that person: what they wear, who they befriend and what they say or do.

When this client went into the local town shopping with a girlfriend, she would receive numerous phone calls from her boyfriend asking where she was and when she was coming back. He would also pour scorn and derision on her if she had any opinion which contradicted his own.

Things came to a head when they had a social evening with two other couples at their house. The more her boyfriend drank, the louder he became. At 9 pm he turned to her and, in front of their friends, said, 'I've had enough of you now, go to bed.' The tragic thing is – she did.

This is where people-pleasing invites in abusers and takers with potentially extreme consequences. People-pleasers are nice people and because of this, they want everything around them to be nice, in the expectation that others be nice back to them. They struggle to understand why others want control over them, and therefore don't see it coming. Everyone is given the benefit of the doubt as they look for the good in people. People-pleasers prefer to lose out themselves, rather than see others suffer.

Another client of mine had won a small contract from a multi-million-pound corporate giant. In order to fulfil that contract, he took on an extra member of staff whom he paid through his own company.

One month on, and the corporate giant hadn't sent any work through for them to get started on, however my client had still incurred set-up costs as well having to pay the salary of his new employee. In all fairness, the corporate client recognised the situation and told my client to invoice them for all his costs. However, as a people-pleaser, wishing to be liked and respected by his corporate master, my client wanted to return a percentage of this payment in order to show good will. I strongly advised him against this, pointing out that it represented a show of weakness and vulnerability, not strength. The corporate payment to him was fair, enabling both parties to uphold their high values through accepting this proposal.

These are just a couple of examples of the blocks that people impose on their lives when they put others first. As people-pleasers, they will do anything and everything to make sure others don't suffer, even if it means suffering themselves, as they want desperately to retain their image as good people. A people-pleaser accepts what others say without contradiction or complaint.

As I grew as a person, I learned that I would be walked all over if I didn't speak up for myself, even if that meant having to complain or contradict someone.

You can start small by speaking up when you disagree with something a person has said: *Don't let others go ahead of you in a queue; Don't let others talk over you in a conversation; Don't agree with another point of view just to be nice.*

These are the simple tests you can try out in order to dilute your need to people-please and start growing your own self-worth. Then you can start standing up to the bigger issues.

I knew I had stopped being a people-pleaser the day one of my rental properties was visited by a council inspector and his boss, when I was looking for a licence as a form of accreditation. By reputation, these visits are known to be difficult and some of the inspectors like to stamp their authority on landlords with all manner of veiled threats. From the moment I met the council officials, I could tell they were 'out to get me', so to speak. The inspector went to one of the toilets and flushed it three times in quick succession. 'Are you actually trying to make that not work?!' I asked him, standing my ground.

He didn't like my direct accusation, but said nothing to my face. Indeed, very little was said to me face-to-face, however I later received a letter raising all sorts of questions over my suitability as a landlord, with criticism of both me personally and my property.

The old people-pleasing Geoff would have kept his head down, avoided conflict and simply satisfied all the conditions that were apparently required in order to provide me with a licence. But not this time. I wrote an equally damning letter back, describing how the inspectors had tried desperately to find fault, but failed to find anything actually wrong.

I also questioned the value of the visit when no criticism was raised face-to-face, with matters only being brought to the table later, from the 'safe comfort' of the council offices, where suddenly accusations were flying thick and fast.

Suffice to say I received a letter of apology and since that time I've had a most productive relationship with these people!

The point I'm making is that I could so easily have been the victim in this scenario, acquiescing to the inspector's unreasonable demands and, as such, giving them tacit permission to behave like this to others.

When you know your values and beliefs, when you know you are doing the right thing, it is your responsibility to say and do what needs to be said and done. Look at it this way, no one learns through people-pleasing behaviour and the victim simply feels worse about themselves.

When you confront the truth, both parties – hopefully – learn that behaviour adjustment is required, and both parties learn to be better people. I learned from my own period of coaching that you will never teach anybody to behave differently if you always go along with them. In terms of my relationship with Derek, he never learned to be any different because I never challenged him or confronted his behaviour. Worse than that, as a people-pleaser I *enabled* his behaviour.

Being a people-pleaser cost my mother the chance to be a nurse all those years ago. When she was told by that stern matron that she wasn't made of the right stuff to work in nursing, she accepted it without question. Pushing back at the authority of the matron would have been unthinkable, especially with her own mother sitting beside her. In my mother's eyes, it was better to accept her fate than cause upset by standing up for what she really wanted out of life.

When we people-please, we allow the views of others to overshadow our own, until we lose our identity and the conviction of our own beliefs. My mother's chief concern would have been keeping her own mother happy who, in turn, would have been concerned only with keeping the matron happy.

A particular trait in people-pleasers is that they venerate bankers, doctors, lawyers and other professionals, putting them on a pedestal. This was especially true of my mother when it came to the medical profession. When my father was ill in later life (he went from being a sickly teenager to being a sickly adult and then a very sickly old man) the doctor told my parents they were conducting a new research programme and would like to trial some drugs on him, if he would allow it.

When my mother told me this, I felt really annoyed. *He's sick enough as it is,* I thought, *don't experiment on the man! What if it has a detrimental effect? He doesn't have the immune system to fight it.* As far as I was concerned, it was a no-brainer to refuse. My parents, however, agreed to the trial and my father was duly started on a new drug which, while it didn't finish him off, certainly didn't make him any better. This was another example of my parents paying any price in the name of people-pleasing: *Oh, he's a doctor, we must do as he asks.* If someone was an expert in anything, my parents never questioned them.

As I've already said, in order to change people-pleasing behaviour, you need to start small. This could be with anything in day-to-day life, for example ordering dinner in a restaurant. If your meal is cold or not up to scratch, say so.

Send it back, ask for it to be reheated or get a refund.

Breaking the habit of people-pleasing might also mean turning down a request for a favour. One client I worked with was so busy that she often felt overwhelmed because she would say yes to anything and everything that was asked of her. *Can you pick up my prescription from the chemist? Sure. Would you collect my children from school for me? Of course... and so on.*

We started small, with me encouraging her to say no. She found this incredibly difficult as she was convinced that saying no made her a bad person – it didn't! When her mother-in-law needed a ride to the hospital, there were other family members far better placed to help out, so I told her to politely decline. She also had two sisters who let her take on the majority of the family support when they were perfectly capable of stepping in themselves.

Start by doing one thing a week; it's not until you flex that muscle that you'll see nothing bad happens when you say no, and no one thinks any less of you.

Another client of mine, who owns a music fan club, worked extremely hard planning a huge music event at a holiday resort, then found herself landed with complaints when the accommodation wasn't up to scratch.

Rather than pass the comments onto the holiday resort staff whose responsibility it was, she chose to compensate attendees out of her own money, so as not to bother anyone or cause a fuss.

A common feature of people-pleasers is accepting poor service and shoddy goods in the name of keeping the peace, rather than risk a confrontation. Fear of conflict is rife amongst people-pleasers. I myself have been guilty of settling for second best, rather than speaking up and risking upsetting someone.

People-pleasers are also apt to hide their political leanings, tv preferences and the sporting teams they support, preferring to 'sit on the fence' rather than voice an opinion that opposes others. Their thinking is, *I'll pretend that I'm the same as you.* That was me all over, accepting poor workmanship to maintain a nice atmosphere, and losing my sense of identity in the process.

You must respect yourself, your beliefs, your opinions and your individuality. Put it like this – if you and I were both exactly the same, one of us would be superfluous!

~ 12 ~

Don't Have a Fixed Mindset
(Anyone Can Change)

Human beings are works in progress that mistakenly think they're 'finished'. The person you are right now is as transient, as fleeting and as temporary, as all the people you've ever been. The one constant in our lives is change.

Professor Daniel Gilbert
Psychologist and author of *Stumbling on Happiness*

When our lives aren't going in the right direction, we have a tendency to accept this as our fate. We tell ourselves and others: *That's just who I am, or, you have to take me as you find me.* In other words, people believe they are fixed and cannot change.

When I was still at school, I told my father that I wanted to study economics and go into business. 'But Geoff, you're no good at maths,' he said. 'You're going to find economics a real struggle.'

This was my father, a parent, and don't we as younger people always think our parents are wise and have the right answers? I therefore took on his judgement – and the identity of someone who might struggle to become a businessman. I didn't take up the option to study economics. It never crossed my mind to challenge my father's comment or work to prove him wrong.

Had I not been able to change this mindset, my life would have continued in the belief that I was 'no good' at something and I would never have changed my career from teaching to sales. In turn, I would never have grown a print business from nothing to seven figures; from there, I would never have built up my very successful property portfolio, nor would I have entered the life-coaching arena.

Despite my father's judgement, I went on to become a very successful businessman – without studying economics. I learned that human beings are not fixed in one identity. The heavenly conveyor belt of babies doesn't roll out another new human being into the hands of its parents with a label zapped into the DNA saying: *Happy and Successful Human Being;* next: *Unhappy Failure;* next…

We're not divided into winners and losers, and yet sadly that's how some people think.

This notion of being 'fixed' begins in childhood, when labels get put on us which we wear until they become part of our identity. I remember my two brothers and I visiting our grandmother when we were quite young, and her telling us, no doubt in a light-hearted way, that within the family I was 'the academic', my middle brother Gary was 'the sportsman' and my youngest brother Richard was 'the creative' one.

Being a sensitive child, I wore that label throughout my childhood, albeit reluctantly, closing my mind to other possibilities and shunning opportunities until I had shaped myself into the person my family expected me to be. Indeed, despite this being a throwaway remark by my grandmother, my two brothers have, to varying degrees, followed paths which validated her judgement of us.

Often, when a judgement is made in this way, we seek out validation in everything around us until it becomes a self-fulfilling prophecy. If we're told not to think of a white elephant, that is exactly the image we conjure, so when we're called out for being, say, shy or introverted, our minds tell us; *Oh yes, that's who I am, I'd better behave in that way to stay safe and stick with how other people see me.* We then find ways to be 'shy and introverted', even if that's not who we want to be.

This is where parenting and teaching methods and styles are so crucial in influencing how a child will grow and develop. Follow the dictum of judging a child's actions, but not their character; point out and correct bad behaviour, but don't invalidate the child for who he or she is.

Another example of my adopting a fixed behaviour as a child was that swimming lesson where I struggled so hard to get my first badge. I heard the phrase, 'Geoff has asthma, so he's not a swimmer,' repeated so often, that I soon saw myself as 'Geoff Who Has Asthma and Therefore Cannot Swim.'

Some schools in the US have taken the lead in not labelling children by introducing 'mastery-based learning' as a means of rewarding progress rather than innate ability.

At Brooklyn's Middle School 442, there is no failing – you simply learn the material sooner or later. ['A New Kind of Classroom: No Grades, No Failing, No Hurry', *The New York Times;* nytimes.com] Instead of kids being graded a 'fail', they are graded a 'not now', meaning they simply need more time and effort to get to where they need to be.

This innovative approach to teaching is visible in a sixth-grade math class, where signs around the room reinforce the school's philosophy: 'Failing proves that you are trying', reads one, while another states, 'Being wrong is the key to being successful'.

In this way, the labels which could have put a child 'in a box' and haunted them for the rest of their lives, are simply never created. How I wish this system had been in place when I was a child!

Were you labelled as a child?

*Did your family set an identity for you which you
didn't wish for yourself?
Have your behaviours and habits ended up
validating that identity, keeping you trapped at a
long distance from your hoped-for destination?*

Then hear it from me – it's a lie. You don't have to wear a label and conform to a set identity. You have all you need to call out that lie and be who you wish to be. I've done it and those I've worked with have done it. We are not fixed. That should be a wake-up call to any human being who is not happy with themselves or their lives.

You can change.

Rest assured that I haven't picked this point out of the ether simply to motivate you – there is science behind the theory, which goes like this: The intrinsic physicality of a human being dictates that our bodies are in a constant state of regeneration and renewal: skin, eyes, hair, and indeed internal organs, are changing all the time – nothing is fixed for life.

The surface layer of our skin (the epidermis) is renewed every two to four weeks, and if a surgeon took away 70% of your liver in an operation, 90% would have grown back in under two weeks.

About 330 billion cells are replaced daily, equivalent to about 1 per cent of all the cells in our bodies. In 80 to 100 days, 30 trillion will have replenished, that's the equivalent of a new you.

[www.scientificamerican.com/article/our-bodies-replace-billions-of-cells-every-day]

The universe itself is in a constant state of flow, in fact, everything is energy and flow. This fundamental theory in the science of 'quantum physics' examines the behaviour of matter and energy (for example atoms and subatomic particles) at a very small scale. In this realm, classical Newtonian physics no longer holds true, and instead we must rely on the principles of quantum mechanics to understand the underlying nature of reality.

The nature of quantum mechanics suggests that everything exists in a state of constant flux and change and that there is no fixed, immutable reality. Instead, the universe is always evolving and adapting. The energy and matter that make up the universe are constantly shifting and changing, changes which are driven by the interactions of particles and waves.

This includes the identity of human beings. Think back to when you were two years old – have you changed since then? Of course you have, and I'm having a laugh here, but if you take this idea to less extreme lengths and look back, say, one or two years, in what ways have you changed in that period of time?

The point I'm making is that while we humans can look back and see that we are now different from our past selves, we really struggle to project forward into the future. We find it hard to process the idea that we have, deep within us, the power to create our future selves. If we want our lives to look a certain way then the time to start is *now!*

Neuroplasticity is another branch of science which supports the notion that as human beings we can rewrite our thought patterns and behaviours. It suggests that the nervous system can change its activity in response to intrinsic or extrinsic stimuli by reorganising its structure, functions, or connections after injuries, such as a stroke or traumatic brain damage. ['The Impact of Studying Brain Plasticity', Pedro Mateos-Aparicio and Antonio Rodriguez-Moreno, *Frontiers in Cellular Neuroscience,* 2019]

Here are two, albeit extreme, examples of neuroplasticity in action:

Phineas Gage was a railroad construction foreman in the 19th century who suffered a severe brain injury when a tamping iron accidentally went through his skull, damaging his prefrontal cortex. Before the injury, Gage was described as a responsible, dependable, and hardworking person. However, after the injury his personality changed dramatically and he became impulsive, unreliable and irritable. This case is significant in the study of brain injuries because it demonstrates the role of the prefrontal cortex in regulating behaviour and personality.

Furniture salesman Jason Padgett suffered a severe concussion after being attacked outside a bar. After the injury, Padgett started to see the world in a completely different way, becoming obsessed with identifying patterns and complex mathematical shapes in everything around him. Padgett went on to become a self-taught mathematician and published a book about his experiences titled *Struck by Genius*. The book which inspired me to uncover more about this phenomenon was Norman Doidge's *The Brain That Changes Itself*.

These examples of neuroplasticity 'in action' are more extreme than the processes linked to personal growth coaching, however they serve to demonstrate the brain's ability to change.

Having read Norman Doidge's book, I was later introduced to Vikki Faudel, whom I've already spoken about. Together with a chiropractor and a neurologist, Vikki created the Neuroplasticity Activation Technique, or NAT, a non-invasive method of working on the prefrontal cortex in order to facilitate positive change.

I was honoured to be one of the chosen few to study this technique, firstly as Vikki's client, and later as a fully-fledged practitioner. Having experienced many different self-improvement techniques, NAT is undoubtedly the one which brought about the deepest and longest lasting positive changes in myself and others. It allowed me to move away from the control of Derek, my ex-business partner, and escape the business I had grown to hate.

The following two case studies highlight just how effective the NAT method can be.

The first is a teenage girl who, having been bullied at school, moved onto college only to find herself in the line of attack once again. Following just three consultations using the NAT method, however, not only was she able to address her 'victim mentality' which stopped the bullying almost at once, she then went on to be an incredible success story.

Another, more extreme example, involved a client I'll call 'Tommy', with whom I worked while I was in the US with Vikki Faudel. In fact, Tommy was initially one of Vikki's clients, however, with her uncanny 'sixth sense', Vikki soon recognised that he wasn't responding to her in the way she hoped and decided that it would be a good idea for me to support him. (Vikki could determine that some clients responded better to male rather than female support, and vice-versa.)

Tommy had suffered terrible abuse at the hands of his mother and stepfather as a child, and was now struggling to overcome this trauma as an adult. His main fear was that he would become an abuser, like his parents, and this impacted his relationships to the point he had convinced himself he would never be able to live happily with a partner.

During one of our sessions, he described a pivotal moment which defined the environment of abuse in which he had grown up:

Aged 11, Tommy would ride his bicycle to and from school every day. One evening, he arrived home and noticed he had a puncture and, knowing he needed his bicycle for his paper round the next morning, he hurriedly wolfed down his tea then told his mom he had some work to do.

Tommy wasn't allowed in his stepfather's workshop without permission, but he disregarded this house rule and took his bicycle into the garage where he fixed the puncture using his stepfather's tools.

Satisfied that he had done a good job, Tommy then stowed his bicycle away and went off to his bedroom to enjoy some downtime.

Two hours later, Tommy's stepfather returned from work. Following his usual routine, he washed his hands and sat down to the meal his wife had carefully prepared for him. Having watched the tv news, he announced that he was off to his garage to work on the classic car he was restoring, he soon noticed that someone had been using his tools.

'Get your ass down here NOW!' he shouted to Tommy who, knowing how short-tempered his stepfather could be, hurried down the stairs.

There followed a tirade of yelling and cursing as Tommy's stepfather demeaned and abused the frightened boy with the following outbursts:

'How many times have I told you not to come down here and use my tools?! Look at how mad you've made me! Why do you always have to push my buttons?! It's your fault that I'm going to have to punish you!'

Moments later, a searing scream of pain rang out across the neighbourhood. 'Help me. Please someone, help me!' cried Tommy, as his father grabbed his hand and dragged him over to the vice.

Some of the neighbours were rooted to the spot, frozen by the blood-curdling scream, however two people close by came running over to see what had happened. They found Tommy with his hand firmly trapped in the vice on his stepfather's workbench. A hammer lay to one side which had been used to smash down on Tommy's hand and break as many bones as possible.

The neighbour quickly freed Tommy's hand from the vice and called 911. At this point, his mother finally arrived on the scene. The first words out of her mouth were: 'Well, you know better than to be using your stepfather's tools — look what you've made him do!' which reinforced the assertion that young 11-year-old Tommy had somehow caused this vicious attack simply by using some garage tools to fix his bike.

This horrendous event labelled Tommy not only as a victim of abuse but also, in his mind, as a potential abuser. This identity was then validated in the short term by his relationships, the work he did and the people he surrounded himself with. More than anything, he feared he'd abuse others, or would form relationships with people who would abuse him.

During the early part of his adult life, Tommy attempted to dull the pain with prescription drugs, weed and alcohol. He then found a partner whom he married, however the self-fulfilling prophecy played out as she was an abuser and his mental health deteriorated to a new low.

This is where so many people end up trapped, finding themselves living the life they've tried so hard to avoid, lured in by the familiarity of their childhood experience. Tommy was used to abuse, and being a victim had become his identity. As such, it was the only future he could see for himself.

It's hard to know exactly how Tommy's life would have continued, had he not been introduced to Vikki Faudel and her NAT method. Fortunately, through a combination of working with her, and subsequently with me, he realised he had to divorce his first wife thus ending his relationship with abuse.

I can happily report that, having worked to clear his negative learned patterns, Tommy was able to change his identity and is now in a loving, committed and caring relationship, in which abuse has no part to play.

Tommy's case was an extreme example, and yet he was able to change himself – and his life. If he can do it, so can you.

If you want to change, you can make it happen. There are methods out there to support and facilitate your desire to change. You are not fixed. Neither are you trapped, nor stuck.

If you only take one thing from this book, then I hope you will take the point that you deserve the best from your life and that your past does not determine your future.

Over a period of about 18 years, I have witnessed people moving from debt to abundance; and from existing in abusive relationships to finding love. Losers have become winners, and those on the brink of despair have found, firstly hope, and secondly, an appreciation of who they are and what their lives consist of, leading ultimately to happiness.

Negative patterns, such as anger, depression, stress and low self-esteem can be removed and replaced by peace of mind, joy, acceptance and self-love. Indeed, both Vikki Faudel and I used this very process to take Tommy from a life of damnation to one of salvation.

I know in my bones that people can change. If you've ever felt stuck, then I hope you will heed my words and seek help. If you don't know where to start, email my support team at support@blankcanvastraining.com

* * *

In recent years, there has been a significant shift in the psychology of personal growth, from delving into the past and raking over earlier traumas, to what is termed in psychology as 'prospection' – the science of looking forward into the future.

Who do you want to become? You are the sculptor of the life you desire, moulding the clay of your identity to shape your future into whatever you want it to be.

Research shows that intentional effort can lead to changes in personality trait. Wagner and Lüdtke *[Personality Change from Life Experiences: Moderation Effect of*

Personality Traits by Wagner and Lüdtke (2020)] explore how various life experiences influence personality change.

This study found that intentional efforts to engage in new experiences and acquire different skills led to positive shifts in personality traits, particularly in those domains related to openness and conscientiousness. However, it's important to note that the extent and nature of personality change may vary across individuals and depend on different factors, such as motivation, persistence, and the specific traits being targeted.

We can actively change negative behaviours or thought patterns by replacing them with positive ones. For example, a person who is naturally pessimistic can intentionally focus on the positive aspects of their life and reframe negative thoughts into more positive ones.

In terms of my own experience, my family was very musical, at least on my mother's side, where I had an uncle who was a lecturer in music. When I started grammar school at age 11, I decided that I wanted to learn to play the flute. Off I went to my first lesson, only to be told by the music teacher that I didn't have a 'musical bone' in my body. So, of course, I abandoned the idea. I'd been given the label 'Geoff Who Is Not Good at Music' and I embraced it.

Fast forward to many years later, when my printing business was due to receive the 'Digital Print Business of the Year' award, and I knew I would have to give an acceptance speech. I looked around for someone who could help me improve my presentation skills and found Angela Caine – a marvellous woman at the Voice and Body Centre in Southampton. She sold herself as a presentation and singing coach, although it certainly felt more like singing coaching to me.

We did all kinds of strange voice exercises, rolling around the floor and bellowing things out. All very weird and wacky, but great fun. The important thing is, Angela believed in me. As we progressed, I discovered that music really touched something in me. It's hard to describe, but it brought out a part of me I didn't know existed.

I hadn't visited Angela to learn to sing, but I discovered my voice – well, *she* discovered my voice – in the process. When she put on a performance at a theatre in Romsey, I sang 'Ich grolle nicht' from Robert Schumann's Dichterliebe song cycle and Irving Berlin's, 'Let's Face the Music and Dance'.

It was quite an emotional night because I sang with my daughter, who was only nine at the time. I received rapturous applause from the audience of around 50 people and I thought, *I do actually have a musical bone in my body!* Indeed, my daughter who carried some uncertainty over her musical ability, also had her talent validated that night. Had I remained fixed with my 'non-musical' identity, I would never have considered taking up any form of music again, and in turn would never have known the elation of performing with my daughter in front of an audience.

This is the sad thing about being told something negative about yourself, then believing it – often for the rest of your life. We see ourselves as fixed with this particular identity, skill set, or personality trait, and fear moving away from it because we believe it defines us. It is who we are: *If I'm not someone who can't swim/sing/start a business/have a successful relationship – then who am I?*

In the same way that I believed I was someone who wasn't musical, after my footballing injury I believed I was someone who would never be active in sport again. I've already talked about self-help author Dan Millman *(of The Peaceful Warrior fame)* who became a very influential mentor in my life, not least because an early experience of his really resonated with me.

Dan was training to be a world champion gymnast in the US when he was involved in a serious motorbike accident, suffering 40 breaks to his leg. When surgeons told him his career as a gymnast was finished, he turned to the world of personal growth and self-development, experimenting with some unconventional methods to help his mental and physical recovery. In particular, he tried martial arts, tai chi, massage, and other 'alternative' methods of regaining his strength and ability and – guess what – he went on to win gold at the Olympics. This turnaround of events is documented in the movie of his life, *The Way of The Peaceful Warrior.*

Reading Dan's book at around the time of my own accident lit a spark in me, and I was so inspired by his example that I enrolled on his courses in California for two years running. During this period, I got to know him well and learned on a deeper level that I was not a fixed entity, and that my life was not fixed on one trajectory. I had choices, I just had to decide what I wanted my future to look like.

Dan's story is a really great example of a person refusing to be fixed. Had he listened to the surgeons and accepted his label of someone who could not be a gymnast, he wouldn't be the successful individual he is today.

Dr Carol S. Dweck is another authority in the 'how humans can change' arena. In her seminal work, *Mindset – Changing the way you think to fulfil your potential,* she explores the difference between a fixed mindset and a growth mindset. She emphasises that individuals with a growth mindset believe that abilities and intelligence can be developed through dedication and hard work, while those with a fixed mindset believe that their abilities and intelligence are fixed traits that cannot be changed.

Those with a fixed mindset tend to give up very easily if progress in their endeavours is slow, as they believe they are either 'good' or 'bad' at something, and this cannot change. In turn, their opportunities in life diminish as they remain trapped in an identity which isn't necessarily who they are.

Those with a growth mindset, on the other hand, might have an aim in life and if progress is slow, they understand that they need to learn more and put in more effort in order to develop. Through persistence and consistency of action, growth mindset individuals ultimately get to where they want to be. They believe that any struggle or failure is nothing more than a temporary signal that they need to continue learning, and that adversity and bumps in the road are there to help them grow and improve. They don't pay too much attention to setbacks.

Sadly, those with a fixed mindset readily give up on their goals if they appear hard to attain and thus find themselves in a perpetual state of looking for the easy option – this can be in business, relationships, or any area of their lives. They look for the path of least resistance, the thing that they don't have to work at. Then, because this rarely exists, they spend their lives swinging between the hope that their next venture will go without a hitch, and consequent disappointment when faced with challenges and obstacles.

As a boy growing up, I would definitely put myself in the category of 'fixed mindset', believing that if something was a struggle, then clearly it wasn't meant for me and I was never going to be any good at it.

Work at something? Improve? My thinking was always that I was only ever going to be good at the innate skills I was born with, so there was no point in putting any work in elsewhere. I did well in the school subjects where I didn't need to put in much effort, and played truant or messed around in those subjects that required extra work.

A growth mindset doesn't rely on pre-ordained

intelligence, it works hard to get better and improve. It thinks: *I'm interested in this. I want to get better at this, so I'll read more about it, maybe seek out the experts and go to a workshop.*

If it's a given fact that you are going to change, and that your life is going to change, wouldn't you prefer to be the driver of that change than be buffeted about on the winds of fate? Wouldn't you rather be the creator of your own destiny?

I'm here to tell you that you *can* be!

~ 13 ~

We Are the Sum of Our Habits

Change your habits to change your life.

Many people want to change but believe it's impossible; the idea that we can change our habits, and in the process rid ourselves of the identity these habits have created for us, gives rise to a lot of fear. Change can feel like the hardest thing in the world to achieve.

The main fear is linked to this idea of losing ourselves: *If I change, I'll lose who I am and become this totally different self, and I don't want that.* We convince ourselves that the habits that form our identity protect us, keeping us secure and comfortable in the knowledge that we understand who we are in a kind of, *I know who I am, warts and all, way.*

In other words, this fear translates into the idea that we will lose sight of who we are and become a totally different self. We worry that if we change beyond recognition, our family and friends will feel differently towards us and not want to spend time with us; in short, they might not love us anymore.

Another fear we have is along the lines of: *Am I going to have to undergo some really painful transition into this new self? What will the fallout be?* We see an unbridgeable chasm between the person we are now, and the person we want to be – and the only way across is to change.

So how *do* we begin to affect the changes we want to see in our lives? The answer is straightforward: one step at a time – or rather, one habit at a time. Lao Tzu summed it up perfectly when he wrote:

Watch your thoughts, they become your words;
watch your words, they become your actions;
watch your actions, they become your habits;
watch your habits, they become your character;
watch your character, it becomes your destiny.

Changing your life by changing your habits, one step at a time, isn't difficult in itself:

1. Decide which habit to change.
2. Take action.
3. Don't look back.

Habits are contagious – they grow (positively or negatively) like knotweed. Take, for example someone who keeps in shape physically and eats healthily, not just to maintain a good physique, but to cultivate a positive mindset. This might involve a daily trip to the gym, eating a clean diet, not drinking alcohol, getting to bed early and rising early. These positive habits create a positive mindset. But what happens if this person spends a week away on a business trip, drinking with clients, eating the 'wrong foods', staying up late and having no time to visit the gym? Back at home, it's easy to continue staying up late, scrolling on a phone, watching trashy tv and eating takeaways. We quickly become the sum of our habits – good or bad.

Our habits can define us, so we need to take control, one step at a time; start back at the gym, put the phone away at night, leave the alcohol…

In terms of the financial arena, clients often come to me with 'money problems' which, straightaway, I can see have grown and flourished from the seed of bad habits. The habit of ordering on Amazon is particularly rich soil!

I currently have a client who is in a considerable amount of debt. She tells me she owes money to her mother, to what she calls 'collections' in the US, and, chiefly, from spending on Amazon, yet she can't stop those deliveries coming. The effect of this uncontrolled spending is that she feels a failure. Similarly, the person who breaks his habits of healthy eating, getting up early and going to the gym, starts to see all the good things in his life: his positivity, his motivation, even his business success, slip away.

Clients will tell me: *I can't get up early in the morning; I can't get to bed early enough; I can't stop scrolling through Facebook; I can't put my phone away...* As all these habits stack up and take control, a person's image of themselves becomes lower. The inner critic that I talked about in Chapter 10 kicks in and says, *You're a loser, what a waste of space you are, you're no good.* This is what I mean when I say that habits are contagious – they spread into every area of your life.

My client with the money problems also had problems with untidiness and poor relationships, to the point that she was living her whole life in chaos. When that happens, we can drift into becoming a 'chaotically-minded person', wasting time looking for things we can't find, going off track in conversations, providing seven answers to a straightforward question when only one is required. We lose clarity of thinking.

The message I want to get across in this chapter is this: when you want to change your life, as we have seen in previous chapters, you have to create a new 'you'. The first port of call in creating that new you is to change your habits.

Taking one habit at a time and changing it from one which hurts you or makes you less, to one which benefits you and increases how good you feel about yourself, can have an incredibly positive effect on all aspects of your happiness and success.

The accumulation of self-destructive habits is something I can relate to in my own life, and is something I've had to work at to overcome. I've had to remove the fear of failure which had become an ingrained habit, halting my progress at every turn.

Habits like this don't just suddenly vanish. You need to work on one level until you feel more confident and happier with who you are and who you are becoming; your view of yourself is enhanced. Then another test from the universe will come into your life and you will deal with it, moving you up another level or two.

I don't want this to sound like a chore, because it isn't. It's actually energising and invigorating as you start to do things you never thought you could do, and become the person you always dreamed of becoming, but didn't think you could.

I enjoyed massive high points when I took on the positive habits of a successful businessman and grew the print company from nothing to over seven figures.

In order to become the person I wanted to be, I looked towards wealthy, successful business people and their habits, and worked out what I needed to do:

1.   I became a five o'clock in the morning person, getting up early to start my days with momentum.

2.   I researched which vitamin and food supplements would best enhance and increase my energy levels as I knew that I would be working long hours in order to grow my business.

3.   I went to bed early in order to fulfil point number 1; getting up early.

4.   On Sunday afternoons I didn't drink any alcohol. I ensured my car was polished, clean and full of petrol as I often had clients or prospects travelling in my car to lunch or to inspect our print factory.

5.   I learned all I could about time management and how to ensure I was working on the most important thing at any given time.

6.   I carried water, a flask of coffee and some fruit or healthy snacks with me as I didn't always have time for lunch and needed to keep my energy levels up throughout the day (and sometimes through the night when I was overseeing one of the massive production jobs that we won).

All the above are the habits of a successful businessperson, and once these habits are incorporated into your routine, you will act and feel differently. You'll feel good, stride forward with your life and become the epitome of success, health, wealth and happiness – this is exactly how I felt when I practised good habits.

Then, when my working relationship with Derek started to break down, leading me to become disillusioned and lethargic about the business, everything changed. When Derek's only thoughts were about his retirement, effectively squashing my ambitions for the future of the business, my habits began to deteriorate and didn't serve me well at all.

I started staying up too late at night watching tv, then struggled to get up in the morning. I grew tired of commuting from Southampton to Guildford for business meetings, and consequently I'd leave late, get stuck in traffic, then have to put a call in to my secretary asking her to push the meeting back because I was running late – yet again.

Getting up late in the morning also meant that I missed breakfast. I didn't carry any of the back-up essentials that I kept with me during my successful years, so by about four o'clock in the afternoon, I'd seek out any sugary snack or greasy fast food I could find in an effort to boost my sagging energy levels. As my days grew more stressful, the unwinding tool of choice would be alcohol. Wine or beer became a crutch for my strained body and mind.

Yes, your positive habits can expand into better and more useful habits so that you live a great life, but the reverse is also true. At this point of my life, my bad habits expanded so that everything suffered. Consequently, my day would start on the back foot and I'd spend the rest of my time playing catch up, with the growing catalogue of jobs I had put off becoming ever more pressing. My habits were contagious, and what began with my disillusionment at work started to grow, seeping out to touch every area of my life.

I had the habits of a failure – and that's how I started to see myself, as a failure. I was lost in a fog, unable to see the a path ahead.

As a coach, I see a lot of people experiencing that same 'fog'; stuck in bad habits, seemingly without a way out. I was very fortunate in that when I went looking for answers, I found Vikki Faudel.

As I've already mentioned, Vikki worked with me using the NAT method. I had begun to doubt everything by this point, telling myself (like a lot of people do when faced with the same situation) that the success with the business had all been down to luck, and had nothing to do with my skills or input.

It is very easy to slide into a real downer on yourself which quickly grows into, I really haven't done much in my life... and starts to snowball.

Success began again for me when I started reverting back to the good habits which had served me so well, helping me make money, grow the business and maintain good health. Most importantly, however, the good habits allowed me to see myself as a successful person who could do anything I wanted to do with my life.

Vikki recognised something in me – I've said that she has an uncanny sixth sense – and it was at this point that she guided me towards coaching others; you could say it was a form of apprenticeship.

When I work with a client face-to-face, either in person or on Zoom, what really strikes me is the change in their physical appearance once they've begun to free themselves from the habits that labelled them as failures. Their skin becomes clearer, their eyes noticeably brighter, and there is just a shine about them that tells me they've found a way out of the fog.

As I learned more about the coaching process and grew my client base, my own habits continued to change. Having a lot of clients overseas meant being on a call in the early hours of the morning, so I changed and adapted my habits in order to do the work I really wanted to do and live the life I really wanted to live. And I would say this: I didn't change immeasurably, I'm still the same Geoff, but – for want of a better phrase – I became a 'better version of myself'.

I'm not saying that you need to get up at four o'clock every morning or make drastic changes – everyone is different – you simply need to take the first step and change the first habit. The rest will improve from there. Look at your habits and decide:

Which habits hurt me?
Which contribute to my feeling bad about myself?
How do I change that?

Some habits are harder to break than others, particularly those linked to food and eating. In these cases, the key is to lower the bar until you find the level at which you can make a change; it doesn't matter if you start low, you just need to take the first step, however tiny it may seem, then take the next, and the next, and the next.

I've talked before about being a straight-line person, someone who identifies what needs to be done, takes action, then identifies the next step ahead. A lot of people look at the whole picture of their lives and the accumulation of all their habits and think, *Oh my God! This is going to be a horrendous task.* Trust me, it isn't. You need to begin with one small thing at a time and take action – be a straight-line person.

In terms of recognising which habits to change, I'd say that people generally know the answer to that question already, although ordinarily they will keep that knowledge to themselves. There's a saying, 'You're only as sick as your secrets'. Taking that first step often comes down to allowing yourself to be vulnerable, which means expressing the things that you've kept hidden deep inside and don't want other people to know about.

When it came to making changes in myself, one of my goals was to become 'psychologically bullet-proof' – I love that term! But what does it mean? Basically, it means not living in fear. For example, if you have a humiliating experience with a person, you put your foot in it, or if someone says something hurtful, or even abusive, you can think, *Oh well, that happened – move on.* You walk away without carrying it with you. That is the essence of being psychologically bullet-proof. It's a way of saying, that person has the problem, not me, and therefore it doesn't touch me.

Being psychologically bullet-proof is something I frequently work with people to achieve. Of course, we are never going to rid ourselves of fear completely, and there's an element of fear that's useful to us, but we don't want it to dominate and get in the way of our being happy or stop us from living the lives we want to live. It's about 'feeling the fear and doing it anyway'.

We often believe that in wrapping ourselves in the security blanket of our habits, we are cushioned from fear. In other words, we might become comfortable eating certain unhealthy foods or drinking a bottle of wine every night in the hope of blocking out fear. However, once we change our habits and find that, actually, we're okay, we uncover a strength in ourselves we didn't know was there. That's when we start to shed the negative identity that's been keeping us prisoner, locked in a fortress built by all those bad habits.

As an example of someone who is psychologically bullet-proof, we can look towards the highest echelons of thinkers, like the Dalai Lama, who is a completely clear vessel. I love the concept of this! A clear vessel is somebody to whom nothing sticks, so nothing hurts them: *Say something really nasty to me and it's the old adage of, it goes in one ear and out the other, it doesn't stick. Pain, plague and pestilence in the world; I can have a love for humanity, but the pain and hurt doesn't stick to me because I'm a clear vessel.*

I used to have acupuncture sessions in London with a Vietnamese monk called Master Thong. He is a wonderful man who still looks about 35, despite being over 70 now! Master Thong is someone to whom I was really drawn, not least because he was into martial arts, like me. I signed up for one of his weekend retreats, then it occurred to me that I needed to give up coffee as I knew the whole retreat would be about good habits and healthy eating, and I didn't want to have a caffeine headache while I was there.

Coffee wasn't an easy habit to break, but despite three or four days of feeling very sluggish, headachy, and generally quite unwell, I decided it was going to be worth it.

We were all at breakfast on the Sunday of the retreat (I'd been there since the Friday) with Master Thong sitting at the head of the table, when he called the waiter over and said, 'Could you bring me over a cup of coffee, please.' I looked across at him, incredulous. 'What's wrong?' he said.

'You drink coffee?!' I replied. 'You don't know the pain I went through before coming here, just so I could give up coffee. I thought it would be all green tea and ginseng!'

He laughed, 'Yeah,' he said, 'I'll have a coffee today, but I might not have another one for three months. Then again, I might have one tomorrow, but I have control over my habits.'

This story really encapsulates what I'm saying in this chapter, which is, in order to change and be the person you want to be, you need to be free from bad habits and addictions. We tend to think of an addiction as being drugs, cigarettes and alcohol, that kind of thing, but being convinced you'll have a bad day if you don't go for a walk, or if you forget to say a prayer, or whatever it is you do… that's still an addiction, especially when it's linked to the belief that breaking the habit will lead you to fail.

When you take a close look at your habits or addictive patterns, think about those you've 'inherited' from your parents and identify the ones that don't serve you anymore. I read recently that the majority of voters in general elections carry on the political alliances of their parents. This demonstrates how we carry our parents' habits forward into our own lives when we become adults.

An example of this is a recent client of mine, Mary, who was in the habit of always putting her washing out on a Monday morning, simply because that's what her mother had always done. The fallout from this habit, however, was that if for any reason Mary wasn't able to put her washing out on a Monday, she felt overwhelmed and unhappy.

It sounds like such a trivial thing, but for her it was a key part of her life. Helping Mary break her Monday morning habit inherited from her mother ultimately helped free her from that enduring and suffocating parental control. That is an important message that I want to get across in this book. When I achieved freedom from my parents' habits: the people-pleasing, the anxiety, the fixed mindedness, I was able to take control of my life. That's when I became successful, achieving all the things my father never could.

Removal of addictive behaviour and freedom from habits all comes back to us being fluid, flowing, and having the ability to change. It's about living a life that doesn't tie us to the wrong habits and doesn't restrict us. Going back to Master Thong, he is the perfect example; he doesn't suffer unhappiness and is what I truly consider to be an enlightened human being.

~ 14 ~

Action Above Everything Else

Everyone is looking for the magic formula to get what they want in life; to realise their long-held ambitions and achieve their goals. But the whole idea of 'living the dream' can seem complicated, distant and for many just that – a dream. The messages on how to become a success are many and varied, and at times the information is so contradictory that we just don't know where to start. Most people hold these dreams in their heads without ever releasing them into existence.

Here's how to turn your dreams into reality...

1.   Decide very clearly what you want and when you want it.

2.   Make a plan of actionable steps that will take you from your starting point to completion of your end goal.

3.   Take an action EVERY DAY (no matter how big or small) so that you are working on your target consistently and daily.

4.   When challenges, doubts, fears and worries occur (and they will) deal with them or call them out as lies depending on whether or not they are real. A real concern, for example, is when you start bringing in more business than you can handle and feel that you're sinking. You must meet this challenge through outsourcing or employing staff – this is dealing with the problem. However, your mind might be telling you to be afraid of your decision to start this business, so you second-guess whether you can make it work and whether it's what people actually want. This is a false fear and you must call out your mind for being a liar and a manipulator.

Write down these fears and doubts and see them as your mind trying to derail and sabotage you. Remind yourself that this was a good idea when you first thought of it and remember that you made a commitment to see these actions through to completion.

Recognise that you're following a familiar pattern of starting out full of enthusiasm for a project, then finding that your motivation starts to wane, leading to your missing firstly one day of action, then two days, then three and so on until, as before, everything starts to trail off.

If you find yourself at this point – stop. Look at your whole plan again and remind yourself why you wanted to do this in the first place. Remember the benefits you identified at the beginning and start taking action again.

Tell yourself that seeing this process through to the end is far more important than the actual final reward of whatever it was you wanted to achieve.

This process, when followed through, teaches you how to get what you want. You recognised that, up until this point, you've always tailed off and stopped doing what you knew you should've been doing. This time it has to be different. If things stay the same, you will live a life of regret and resentment – even shame.

If you're really thinking of throwing in the towel and giving up again, then email me at support@blankcanvastraining.com explaining where you are and how you're feeling and I will ensure you receive some help.

5.   Don't look at the end, just look at the next action. I keep saying this, but it's crucial. Taking the next step in a series of actions is more doable than looking at the whole plan. Be easy on yourself and trust that by completing each step the end result will take care of itself.

6.   Take time to relax. Success, happiness, wealth and good health don't respond well to force. When we force, we become tense, stressed, and even panicked. You need energy to fulfil your dreams, so don't waste it on worry, conserve it for the positive actions you are taking every day. You can be active and busy whilst remaining calm and centred, safe in the knowledge that you're moving towards what you want.

7.   Closely connected to point 6 above is the need to detach yourself from the outcome of this plan. This sounds like a contradiction in terms but hear me out.

Life has a funny habit of showing us humans that we don't control everything – think Covid-19 and climate change. If we only control what is in our power to control, by which I mean our habits and our actions, and let life get on with everything else, not only do we reduce down the pressure on ourselves, we also often find that life presents us with better options than those we'd thought of on our own.

In practically all my endeavours, I set a goal then work towards it. I've been most successful when I've taken action, but then stepped back and allowed life to throw in some unexpected twists and turns. When I detach myself from the events I can't change, then accept, adapt, and tweak my actions accordingly, I find the rewards are bigger and better than I'd imagined in the first place.

For example, when I embarked on my 'property journey' I knew nothing about property, all I had was some spare money which I wanted to invest in bricks and mortar. I set myself the goal of buying a property despite not knowing where, or what type. I knew very little about making money from property, other than setting up a single let to a family. At the time, the whole project was little more than a side hustle and I had just one property to make some money on the side.

Then I saw an opportunity to own a 'house of multiple occupancy' or HMO, whereby rooms are rented out individually to tenants. This proved to be far more lucrative than I could have imagined, but this significant step only happened because I was prepared to follow the new and different path that opened up to me.

I amended my plans and adjusted my actions accordingly, growing a substantial property portfolio, the income from which gave me the freedom not to have to work.

I then began finding properties for other people and coaching them on how to get started with their own portfolios, which provided me with an additional income stream.

By detaching yourself from the outcome of your project and focussing on taking each step – each action – one at a time, you could, like me, find yourself in the very happy position of achieving far more than you initially imagined.

I hope this idea of 'detachment from the outcome' makes sense to you. It really is one of the most powerful weapons in your armoury!

Now you can really appreciate how success boils down to seeking out that first step – and taking it. It's simple but, oh my goodness, the times clients come to me who've gone from hope to disappointment and back again, multiple times. They start, they stop; they change their minds; they procrastinate; they make excuses…

A lot of people who want help with a business will tell me that their goal is to be a 'millionaire' – often in six months! However, I can see that they are nowhere near achieving this in terms of their thinking and their abilities.

Many people quite simply don't really know what they want in life and truly cannot imagine a better future for themselves. They don't trust their dreams and visions, and, consequently, they don't know what they want because they don't believe they will ever get it.

I should add, of course, that there are many people who *are* perfectly happy and content with their lot – who are accepting and fulfilled with all they have – and I salute them. However, there are many more people stuck in the quagmire of mediocrity, yearning for a way out. They either cannot use their imagination, or they don't trust their vision of a desired future.

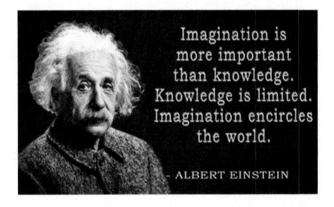

Imagination is more important than knowledge. Knowledge is limited. Imagination encircles the world.

- ALBERT EINSTEIN

Why? Quite simply because of fear. Fear stops them from dreaming. Fear inhibits their vision of a better life. Fear stops them creating a brighter future. An idea might well pop into their head, then fear intervenes saying:

> *Who do you think you are, believing you can do that?*
> *You'll never manage to do that. It's all just too hard.*
> *This is for other people but not for you.*

The first step on the road to recovery is being clear about what you want. There are three important questions into which you must deep dive:

1. *What are you good at?* This doesn't have to be something you're the best in the world at, or some unique, innate skill, just consider where your skillset lies. Is it, for example: selling, speaking, writing? All you need to do is identify something you're better-than-average at doing.

2. *What do you like doing?* Think of something you would enjoy doing, if you weren't being paid.

3. *Is there a market for what you want to do?* Who might want or need what you're offering? How can you make your offering different to anything that has gone before?

The answers to these questions aren't easy because people come at them from a negative, reluctant mind space. If they do profess to having a skill or a particular ability, a debilitating 'imposter syndrome' quickly sets in, which no amount of proof or convincing can drive away.

A client of mine, Yvette, who had been a stay-at-home mother for most of her life, argued against any suggestion of her being good at anything, preferring to stay humble and in the shadows. She particularly disliked showy, arrogant braggards and couldn't see that there's a middle ground between totally denying your God-given talents and being a loud-mouthed show-off.

Through persistent and deeper and deeper questioning, however, we came up with the following positive responses:

1.   Yvette was able to admit that she was very good at organising.

2.   She loved the music of one rock band in particular and had followed them for years, and still attended most of their gigs.

3.   Yes, indeed there was a place for her in the music industry. We brainstormed putting on music events, selling merchandise and memorabilia, reporting on and writing articles about the band. Lots of positive ideas started to flow. Once we had broken down her resistance to the idea, her imagination started to kick in and she suddenly became creative.

In an exciting turn of events, very soon after our constructing this vision of a future project together in her head, I kid you not… the fan club of this famous rock band came onto the market and Yvette bought it!

She went from a woman sitting at home staring at four walls, denying she had anything to offer the world, to giving the fans of this band a value-for-money, expertly run fan club. Not only that, but she has also interviewed the band and had her writing published.

Yvette has also written a memoir. But bigger than any of the above, she has organised fantastic music events, bringing huge pleasure and lasting memories to thousands of people.

Can you see how breaking down resistance, removing fears, doubts and worries, then just getting started on the actions opens up a pathway to everything you want?

* * *

I truly believe that the future wealth due to us as human beings is out there, waiting to be claimed by each individual in line with our innate talents, interests, and personalities. Our success comes not from seeing what others are doing or copying the current trend, our success comes from within. When I coach people on how to reach their goals, I really delve into their psyche and ask, 'What is your pot of gold at the end of the rainbow?' because it's there waiting, you just need to find it.

My pot of gold, and I'm now realising this more than ever, was neither printing nor property, it was about speaking, writing and coaching. *Your* goal, that thing you really want out of life, has to resonate within you, otherwise you'll simply give it up when it doesn't go right.

If that goal seems impossible to reach, like making a million pounds in six months, I tell people to step back from the end result and concentrate on the first step. I might say, 'Could you make £1,000 in three months?' If they still have doubts, I lower the bar until we reach an achievable first step, a first point of action. 'Right, that's our stepping-stone,' I say. 'Do that.'

I tend to use money as an example, but the same strategy applies with dating, health, and basically all arenas in life. It's all about taking that first achievable step: set a goal, plan the action, take the action and complete it. Then you gain a little bit of confidence, then you move onto the next step, and complete it, each time stretching yourself a bit further. The key phrase is *complete it*. Remember: action above everything else.

Naturally, different people will set their goals at different levels, and that's fine. One of my clients gave up a corporate job where he was earning in excess of £100k a year – and hating it! Whilst he had the lovely house, the smart car and lots of material possessions, being under constant pressure was making him very unhappy. His main worry on quitting his job and starting his own business was losing his regular salary, however, I could see he had talent and knew that he was capable of earning a high figure. I usually set goals for completion within a 90-day period, and this client earned

£190k in his first 90 days. It's not *always* about starting small. Everyone has a different level of comfort and self-belief.

In order to achieve our goals, we need to take action one step at a time, always moving forward, however small the step, and never looking back. Be a straight-line person, not a zigzagger who takes one step forward, meets an impasse, then takes a step back; or a circle person, who moves between motivation and apathy without ever achieving anything.

Among my older friends, I see circle people and zigzag people, now spent and exhausted, disillusioned in their later lives, knowing they will never achieve their dreams or reach their goals.

Action trumps thought. And where does all this thinking, circling and zigzagging take place? In your head. As part of my coaching course, I give people a 90-day plan to follow. If someone commits fully to the plan and, after 90 days, it hasn't worked, we make another plan. Either way, we keep moving forward. Just follow: action, action, action. When barriers spring up, push them out the way or work around them.

Take action – don't look back – keep moving forward.

~ 15 ~

Be Inspired

'The two most important days in your life are the day you are born, and the day you find out why.'

Mark Twain

When you clear the 'weeds' in your head, the explanations of life and living become glaringly obvious. In other words, when you are mentally clear there aren't so many conflicting stories vying for your attention. You become more confident that your own inner wisdom has the answers you seek, and you don't need to listen to other people's opinions.

You are the expert on you. Instead of worrying and stressing over unknowns and 'what-ifs', you can almost see the molecular structure of the universe and thereby know exactly what you should do now. You understand that there was a plan which got you to here, and, in recognising that all the really tough moments were actually working *for* you, helping you take massive strides towards what you wanted, you begin to trust life again… and through trusting life, you trust yourself.

My mother desperately wanted to be a nurse but was unable to fulfil that ambition. Last year, after much struggle against life circumstances, my daughter Clare obtained a first-class honours degree in nursing. Where her grandmother heard a 'no', Clare achieved a 'yes', despite having the added challenge of being a single mum to two boys. She overcame this challenge and is now in a nursing position which uses all of her innate skills. She is truly expressing her God-given talent in the world and is very happy.

Coincidence? There's no such thing!

Both my father and I fell short of our ambition to work in the world of football. My son Chris, however, has a job he loves which sees him jetting off all over the place, looking after some of the biggest football clubs in the world.

Coincidence? I think not!

See the pattern?

Have you developed your self-awareness to the point that you are able to join up the dots in *your* life?

Our darkest, most desperate days can guide us towards the next best thing, like cats' eyes shining the way through the fog down the middle of the road. The saying goes that t*he* *darkest hour is always just before dawn.*

Dislocating my ankle and being unable to play professional football was the darkness that 'lit the way' to my finding the world of personal growth. I discovered Dan Millman and, through his writings and eventually his courses, I found a more enlightened way of approaching life.

Another dark episode that ultimately brought me into the light was losing £20,000 to the Postal Centre franchise. Needing money to pay off that debt pushed me out of teaching and into business.

Lastly, and perhaps most significantly, is 'the month that changed my life' - February 2008. This is when I lost my dad, escaped the clutches of my ex-business partner and overcame the armed gunman. *This* was when I really broke out of my life of fear and stress. It was when I saw a clear picture of who I was and what I wanted to do with my life. It was when I finally understood, on a much deeper level, that I could get what I wanted.

Let me ask you this question: If you knew that you could have whatever you wanted out of life, what would you do – right here, right now?

Too many people don't know what they want, and that is their sticking point. Napoleon Hill, in his masterpiece, *Think and Grow Rich,* advises that we must find and cultivate 'definitiveness of purpose'. Once we have done this, he tells us we become unstoppable.

And… for those of you who feel your time has passed

and think that it's too late to find your 'thing' – know that it is *never* too late. There was a time in my life when I was in my early 50's and my advisor on property was just 28 years old. I was also seeking business advice from Jon Street, who must have been 30 at the time, and learning about cryptocurrency from another 30-something, Siam Kidd. Perhaps understandably, I felt an amount of regret and resentment that here were all these younger entrepreneurs giving me – at almost twice their age – the benefit of their wisdom. *Why couldn't I have had a better understanding of life and business at a younger age? I asked myself.*

I know that some of you will have had this form of jealousy show its ugly head. I also know, from experience, that it's not a nice feeling. However, my jealousy was just a fleeting thought and I was able to boot my ego into touch and reframe the situation using Ben Hardy and Dan Sullivan's principle of 'The Gap and The Gain' (described in their book of the same title).

My mind (and especially my ego) was measuring the 'gap' between where I was in my life and where these young 30 year olds were. However, when I reframed my position and looked at the 'gain' I had made from being a simple village boy in Northumberland, with no idea of what he wanted to do in life and believing he had no discernible talent, to where I was in that moment, I was able to take great pride in how far I'd come.

The moral here is that there is absolutely no point in

comparing your life against another person's life. Although as humans we are all connected, remember that a totally different set of circumstances has led each of us to the point at which we now find ourselves. That is to say, we start from different positions, are influenced by different people and affected by different environments. Don't allow jealousy of others to stunt your progress.

Most importantly – know that it is *never* too late. Keep going after what you want.

* * *

As we near the end of this book, it feels right for me to answer the two questions I am most frequently asked by coaching clients: *Do I still experience fear? and Do I still fear failure?*

The answer to both is a resounding 'yes' – which is not what you, or they, want to hear.

If I were the glib social media imposter, posting empty platitudes from wisesayings.com to gain clickbait, of course I'd say that I'm never fearful and don't fear failure. But that would be the kind of BS spouted by those who wish to keep their vulnerability a secret.

Fear and failure, and indeed fear *of* failure, are integral parts of being human and are only dangerous to us when we don't acknowledge them; when we attempt to push them further down inside of us. This is what causes even more damage.

Despite everything I've learned and taught, I do feel these emotions, but only for a very short length of time. When they appear, as they might, I simply call them out and away they go. And that's how it should be, so they do no lasting harm.

Life gives us various contrasting emotions and feelings. Fear, sadness, depression, joy, stress and anger all exist, and most of us have experienced many, if not all of them. So when they appear let them come up, then let them go.

When a baby is hungry, he cries at full force. Once fed, he stops immediately. Our emotions should behave in the same way. Let them come up, and then release them. Watch how a baby's face can switch directly from disgust at putting something horrible in her mouth, to the brightest smile when she experiences something nice immediately afterwards.

For me, the answer is always 'yes' to the idea of trying something new. I might well feel some fear, but I now no longer hang on to it and am not transfixed by it. It doesn't eat me up and occupy my every waking moment, then prevent me from sleeping as it goes round and round in my mind.

It's the same with fear of failure. Yes, it does sometimes enter my mind as I approach a new venture; it's entered my mind whilst writing this book: *What if people don't like what I've written? What if people say it's rubbish?* and, worst of all, *What if no-one reads it?*

But remember – action trumps words, thoughts and

fears. *Just write the book, Geoff. Your mind is trying to keep you safe and stop you from stepping out. Ignore it – just write.* And with that reminder to myself, I just get on with the job in hand.

Peter Thomson, the great British marketing guru, taught me a simple mantra linked to the London postcode SW3:

Some Will.

Some Won't.

So What?

Or, in other words,

Some people Will like you and what you do.

Some people Won't like you and what you do.

So, What do you care?

You have to tread your own path without taking on the judgements of others.

Do what you know, deep down within, you are meant to do.

Don't deny your greatness through fear of what anybody else says about you.

In fact, the bigger and bolder you strive to make your life, the more judgement and criticism you'll experience. Look at how the media, and the general public, have tried to bring down the likes of Bill Gates, Sir Richard Branson and Elon Musk. Yet these great innovators have developed the ability to become 'psychologically bulletproof', rating achievement of their goals far above being liked.

A relative once asked me, 'What do you think is so wrong with you that you have to step out and do all these different things?' His belief was that I had become driven because I was unhappy with who I was and just couldn't accept a normal life. In a way, he was right. But what he didn't understand was that this was my journey, every part of which I was enjoying at the time, and have continued to enjoy. I haven't been working towards an end goal, I'm just enjoying the ride.

Whilst I can't say what constitutes a 'normal' life, I know I've always had the urge to follow my own path and do things my way, independent of limitations and conventions. Not everyone feels the same, and that's okay. My story is to inspire those of you who experience the same inbuilt motivations; those who are struggling to break out of the confines of your family background, your education and/or your environment, while at the same time striving to protect yourself against loss.

When I received that thinly veiled criticism from my older relative, I was undergoing quite drastic orthodontic work to widen my palate, improve my breathing and achieve a better physical balance. Few people I knew could understand why a man in his 50's would want to undergo wearing braces, complete with accompanying dribbling down his chin and lisping when he'd never lisped before. Well, that was just me.

The reality was that I'd been diagnosed as having a tilted pelvis by my chiropractor; a skeletal imbalance which he suggested stemmed from a misalignment in my maxillofacial structure. Me being me, it became my mission to rectify this problem and I spent thousands of pounds, and went through four years of painful treatment, to become a better version of myself.

While the aesthetics weren't necessarily much improved once all the treatment had been completed, I no longer suffered from lower back pain and my strength trainer made the assessment that I was 10% stronger now that my palate was wider. The upshot was that, now in my 50s, my breathing had improved and my general health was better than it had been when I was in my 30s.

This has been the extent of my self-improvement obsession, and also the source of whispers behind my back, as well as some snidey derision. In part, my elderly relative's comment came from a place of sympathy for me and was almost a plea for me to stop and just accept myself as I was.

Some years later, I was in the pub (there's nothing like a drop of alcohol to make the truth appear) when this same relative turned to me and started telling me how he too could have been a businessman – this was at a time when I was enjoying a great deal of success with my print company. He told me how, as a teenager, he'd created a unique design of toy soldier and had begun selling these locally, loving the excitement of starting an entrepreneurial enterprise. He then admitted to a deep regret at not continuing with the business.

Despite a long career in education, which anyone who knew this man would have considered very successful, in that moment he allowed himself to be vulnerable, opening up to me about his disappointment at not stepping up to follow his dream all those years ago. Living well, surrounded by all the trappings of his distinguished career, he was telling me that he should have done more.

That's the feeling which has always driven me on; driven me to do more, be more and have more. It's a feeling that has caused me enormous stress, pressure and fear at times. Indeed, my inherited inborn fear of failure has been the driver, pushing me on when I've wanted to stop.

* * *

I've written a lot about the negatives surrounding the fear of failure, but this fear undoubtedly has a positive side. In my own case, it forced me into taking a new direction away from pain and ultimately towards pleasure. Those of you who have studied personal growth will recognise the two different types of goal incentive: '*towards* motivation' and '*away from* motivation', each of which has the power to effect change in its own right.

Following my footballing injury, I had to change my

life in order to move away from the pain of losing out on my dream job. Similarly, the £20,000 debt I incurred from the Postal Centre franchise provided the *away from* motivation to change the situation, as I was forced to seek out an alternative way of making money.

In terms of *towards* motivation, becoming a top salesman and then starting my own business drove me forward towards something I wanted – a career where I could earn good money. I now had a vehicle facilitating my moving towards personal growth and the ability to control my own destiny, with no ceiling on my potential earnings.

Where are you operating from now? Are you striving to move *away* from pain and struggle, or are you moving *towards* what you want?

There's no doubt that *towards* motivation didn't cause me any stress, tension or fear, whereas *away* from motivation was steeped in pain and suffering.

In consciously working out what you want and moving towards that goal, you are taking the initiative; you are telling the universe what you want to happen. *You* are the starting point – through everything you say, everything you do and everything you think. I urge you to be proactive in your life. Get to know what you want then make a plan setting out how you're going to get there. Ensure every decision you make involves moving in that direction.

'At the moment of commitment, the entire universe conspires to assist you.'

Johann Wolfgang von Goethe

Whenever I've decided to fully commit to something, I find it amazing how the right people appear to make it happen, or the money to invest mysteriously materialises.

I taught my children that chance encounters, previously unthought-of connections, and seemingly random coincidences all ensue once you decide, commit and act. They now see this as normal practice. A wish made at the start of any given year would often come true within a matter of weeks, rather than the anticipated long months.

* * *

I sincerely hope you will have gained something from my story and the things I've learned along the way.

Your life is going to change. *You* are going to change – those are the facts. So wouldn't you rather be the driver of that change, not just a passenger swept along for the ride, buffeted by the whims and fancies of fate? I'm here to tell you that you *can* be the creator. You can be the controller of your own life and its evolution!

I haven't lived a Pollyanna existence. I've known some incredible lows which have brought me to my knees at times, but I've come to understand that wisdom grows from the seeds of these difficult times. You don't become wise living in La-La-Land.

During lockdown I had the incredible experience of working with Dr Leonard Laskow. Dr Laskow is a Stanford-trained Life Fellow of the American College of Obstetrics and Gynaecology, and a founding diplomate of the American Board of Integrative Holistic Medicine. He also served as a US Naval Flight Surgeon in Vietnam.

From this solid scientific medical background, Dr Laskow discovered that he was a healer, obtaining incredible results from his healing methods, especially in the field of cancer. I learned more about his work through reading his book, *For Giving Love,* which is the most influential book I've ever read.

Without going into detail about every aspect of Dr Laskow's philosophy, here are some quotes which give an insight into his teachings. They might help you decide if this way of seeing the world can benefit you:

> *Happiness is a place we are coming from,*
> *not going to.*
> *We are inherently whole. Only the thinking mind*
> *dismembers us from our essence.*
> *The purpose of forgiveness is to release attachment to*
> *the past so that we are free to live and love in the*
> *present.*

Dr Laskow suggests we forgive our past events, our past lives and the people in our past. Most importantly, he says we must forgive our past *selves,* and the purpose of this forgiveness is 'For Giving Love'.

Instead of being this accumulation of f**ck-ups, cockups, shame, blame and criticism, we need to forgive all that has gone before and then, rather than continually breaking ourselves down, we have to build ourselves up and learn to love again.

Indeed, for me, writing this book has been part of a therapeutic process whereby I have distanced myself from the meaningless, trivial hurts and slights I've been subjected to, and have carried with me. I could then forgive myself for thinking I was less than I am.

You, my friend, are much more than *you* ever thought, and my wish for you is that you too will forgive yourself, step into your power, and love yourself wholly and unconditionally.

Above: The swimming certificate that made
me feel like a failure

Below: Coaching at the Wutan School of Martial Arts
(kick-boxing and Kung Fu) in the mid-1990s

Above: Finding peace in Colorado

Below: My children, Clare and Christopher

Acknowledgements

I have always known I would write a book and have been writing drafts since 2019, but without Helen Adlam co-writing, editing and generally keeping me on topic, I don't think I would ever have completed this book - so a massive thank you to her.

I sincerely thank Dan Millman for inspiring me to recover from my footballing injury and for introducing me to a world of personal growth I didn't know existed.

I dread to think where I might be in life if I hadn't met Vikki Faudel. Thank you for taking my blinkers off and showing me who I really was and what I could do.

A massive shout out to all my coaching clients who have put their trust in me to guide and support them to whatever they have wanted to achieve. You inspire me with your incredible success stories.

Thank you to my parents, Arthur and Dorothy, and my brothers, Gary and Richard, for the connection we share.

Thank you Hallie May, Ben and Rory for keeping me young and allowing me to be a child again.

Thank you Christopher and Clare for all the fun, laughter and love we've shared.

And, of course, my amazing wife Sue. You are my best friend, my rock and the love of my life. Thank you for being there for me.

Printed in Great Britain
by Amazon

37675192R00106